Tripping Up

A Cult Memoir
by John Titus

Photos courtesy of *The Family International.*

First Edition: Huge Jam, 2021
Copyright © 2021 John Titus
www.trippingup.net
ISBN: 978-1-911249-63-4

Dedication

To Philip Yancey who called me on the phone
in 1984 and encouraged me to keep my journals
safe because they were history.

Acknowledgments

I would like to thank my wife, Miriam, and my friends,
Kathy and Terry, for faithfully reading my drafts (sometimes
twice) and making many valuable suggestions. I'd also like
to thank Jacqueline Tobin for the work she did in preparing
my manuscript for publication.

Table of Illustrations

Title Page *Bertoldino Falls into the Fish Pond*, Giuseppe Crespi (1701)
Part 1 *The Pied Piper of Hamelin*, Henry Marsh (1868)
Part 2 *The Gingerbread Boy and the Fox*, Miriam (2021)
Part 3 *Peter, Wendy and the Lost Boys,* F. D. Bedford (1911)
Part 4 *Pinocchio*, Enrico Mazzanti (1883)
Part 5 *Puss In Boots*, Pauquet (1843)
Part 6 *Tom Thumb Gets Caged*, unknown artist (1880)
Part 7 *Hansel and Gretel Meet the Witch*, Arthur Rackham (1909)
Part 8 *Red Riding Hood and the Wolf*, Gustave Doré (1862)
Part 9 *Alice at the Mad Hatter's Tea Party*, John Tenniel
Part 10 *Rapunzel Has a Visitor*, H. J. Ford (1812)
Part 11 *Jack Chased By the Giant,* H. J. Ford (1890)
Part 12 *The Princess and the Frog*, Edsel Arnold (edselarnold.com)

1

August 1970 to January 1971

The Piper's music promised a most enchanted land
Full of fun and adventure where life would be so grand
The parents cried aloud with much fear and great concern
But the children couldn't hear them and never returned

THE LOONY BUS

WHEN I WAS A TEENAGER I joined a radical religious cult.

It was kind of like running off with the circus. Of course, I didn't know it was a cult. I thought a cult would be like the Hare Krishnas—you know—the ones that shaved their heads, put on robes and danced around with little drums. Shave my head? No way! That was nuts.

It was 1970 and I was in Austin visiting some friends, hanging out at Zilker Park on a beautiful summer day. All decked out in my customary uniform—white tee shirt, bell bottom jeans, buffalo sandals from India, and a green army surplus shirt with the sleeves ripped off—I blended in well with all the other non-conformist free thinkers. My hair was not as long as I wanted it to be, but I made up for it with my John Lennon glasses.

As I soaked in the groovy vibrations, I saw a line of people wearing red sackcloth robes coming my way. They marched in unison and thumped tall, heavy sticks on the ground. The group abruptly stopped in a clearing and formed two rows. They stood back-to-back, unfurled canvas scrolls, and stared into the air. After a while, curious folks in the park began circling this assembly. For sure I wanted to check it out, so I strolled over.

The quiet around this group was eerie. They were all frozen like statues, still holding their scrolls and big sticks. It was a mix of young people, male and female, about 20 in the group. All of them had ashes smeared on their foreheads and their robes made them look like prophets from the Bible. That was the point, I guess. For a final touch, they wore strange things around their necks—a flexible branch bent into a U shape and fastened to a board about a foot long. Wow! You didn't see this every day.

The scrolls displayed scary Bible verses about judgment and doom—definitely not your standard "Jesus loves you" stuff. As I strolled around the group, trying to make sense of it all, I noticed these guys had regular clothes on under the sackcloth. Most of them looked pretty young, like me. And no joke, some of them had tears streaming down their cheeks. They stayed in that position for a long time—long enough for me to lose interest. But as I wandered off, the prophet people raised their big sticks into the air and shouted, "Woe!" I mean, they really screamed it out. This was repeated three times before they marched off in a cloud of dust.

"The quiet around the group was eerie."

"They ride around in a big bus and park on the main drag."

I watched the spectacle retreat and then walked around to find my friends. When I described what I saw, they told me, "Oh, yeah. Those are the Jesus Freaks. They ride around in a big bus and park on the main drag." Sure enough, when we headed in that direction, there was the bus.

It had a big sign painted on the side: THE PROPHET BUS. FREE FOOD! FREE MUSIC! COME AND SEE! THE CHILDREN OF GOD. And there was a picture painted of a guy holding up a scroll and a stick. Yep, these were the guys from the park. My friends and I promptly dubbed it THE LOONY BUS. So that was my introduction to the Children of God. It would be five months before I saw them again.

My friends and I used the rest of the weekend to smoke grass and pop psychedelics. Then I headed down to south Texas where I lived with my sister. Fresh out of high school, I had not settled on a college. It took me a while because I despised my high school experience and wasn't exactly thrilled about more classes to bore me out of my skull. Besides, I was full of hippie inspiration after reading books written by the Yippie drop out activists Jerry Rubin and Abby Hoffman.

My friends in Austin, with their long hair and moustaches, talked about the city like it was a flower power Mecca. And after spying out the land, I came up with a scheme to move up and give the University of Texas a shot. Perhaps I could combine academics and counterculture. My father agreed with the plan—not the hippie part, but the college part—so I made arrangements to begin classes in Austin at the beginning of 1971.

While I killed time in my sister's house, I couldn't get those Jesus freaks out of my head. They seemed so happy dancing around their bus. But I wasn't interested in the Jesus part. As a good little heathen, I proclaimed I was an atheist. I really wasn't, but it was a good line for the girls who delighted in being shocked and tried to convert me. I also thought it made me seem cool, like I was an intellectual, like I had grappled with the concept of a higher power. The truth was I thought about God as little as possible. The pursuit of pleasure was my goal and God just wasn't convenient. A creator might require something from me or have something to say about my life. Perhaps I would think about God later—after I had some fun.

My high school science books assured me the origin of everything could be explained by matter, time and chance—so nothing to worry about, right? But as I continued on my merry way, pesky God thoughts occasionally popped into my head—especially when I behaved like a dick, which was often. But I didn't know how to change.

I was pretty skilled at excusing my questionable activities. I'd just say to myself, "Hey, that's in the grey zone, man." But when my behavior fell squarely in the black—like after stealing from my family to buy drugs or some philandering sexual escapades—I felt ashamed. Did it mean I was not a "good person" after all?

But then I had a dramatic experience that shifted the tectonic plates of my teenage brain. I was alone in my bedroom with a tab of LSD my sister got from one of her boyfriends (she didn't do drugs and would pass them on to me). She was out on a date and I was on my own for the night. I knew it was a bad idea to take LSD when you are alone, but I risked it. Sure enough, I wound up sprawled out on my bed, totally freaking out. This went on for a while until, at the height of hellish anxiety, I remembered God.

So I prayed, "I really need your help now!"

What happened next is difficult to describe—words are not enough. All of a sudden I became aware of God's presence. Quite simply, I knew God was with me and I was overwhelmed by the love coming my way. It was inserted into my mind and saturated it. One thing became perfectly clear: God loved me with a love beyond anything I thought possible. I was filled with awe and wonder that such a thing was happening to me. This love was far beyond human relationships. I knew I was not worthy and had done nothing to deserve it. But God accepted me despite all my flaws. His love was so real I felt I could reach out and touch it. I burst into tears and asked, *"Why me? Why me?"*

I can't say for sure how much time passed, but it was too intense to have lasted more than a few minutes. When my mind could catch a breath, I was strangely calm and clear-headed, not feeling high anymore. Weird. I went from a bad acid trip to no acid trip. I left the house and walked around in the dark for hours before dawn, repeating a phrase like a chant, "God is love. Love is God." Speaking to God seemed like a natural thing to me now. So I asked, "What am I supposed to do? Show me the way." For some reason I added, *"I don't know if I will be able to do what you want, but please SHOW ME THE WAY."*

Morning came and my sister returned from her night out. I found her in the kitchen making breakfast and told her about my experience with great excitement. She gave me this look like I had just seen the face of Jesus on a piece of burnt toast. When I was done, she smiled sadly and said, "Well, it's been nice knowing you."

Back then I had a friend named Travis. The way we met was kind of interesting. But first let me give you some essential background. In high school I discovered the comedian, Lenny Bruce. In fact, I had most of his material memorized because I listened to his recordings so much. Okay, that sets it up for you. So, one night my sister invited some friends over and introduced Travis, one of the few black guys in our town. Travis and I ended up off in a corner, drinking beer and shooting the breeze. Since he was the only black person at the party, I launched into Lenny Bruce's famous routine entitled HOW TO RELAX YOUR COLORED FRIENDS AT PARTIES.

*"Did you get enough to eat? Sorry we don't have any
fried chicken or watermelon around. (Awkward pause)
That Bojangles... Christ, could he tap dance!"*

As I let it rip, Travis doubled over with laughter. He got it. After that night we hung out regularly, mostly to smoke grass. Weeks later he came over and I told him about my epiphany, my profound experience of God's love. This piqued his interest and we discussed it for quite some time.

"Travis, I don't know what is happening. You know what I like to do best? I take walks and sing to God."

Then Travis said, "Someone told me once that Jesus said *'I am the way, the truth and the life.'* I don't know what that means, but I can't stop thinking about it."

After he left, I couldn't stop thinking about it either. Didn't I ask God to show me the way? And Jesus said, *"I am the way."* I had a good feeling, like I was about to get an answer. I still had the New Testament my mother gave me when I was a child; so I flipped through the pages looking for the passage Travis mentioned—where could it be? For some reason I started with the Gospel of John. Some parts puzzled me while other parts seemed clear. Eventually I came to John 14:6—the verse that started the whole thing. By then something amazing was going on—the more I read, the more I loved Jesus.

I went out and bought a copy of JESUS CHRIST SUPER STAR (a popular Rock Opera). When I listened to the album, I didn't even catch on that the lyrics were putting Jesus down. Rather, I would sit in the dark with my headphones and cried through many of the lyrics, especially when Mary Magdalene sang *"I don't know how to love him."* That song expressed what was going on in my heart:

*"I love you, Jesus, but I don't know how. I've been
changed, but I don't know what to do."*

Since I had refused to go to the church with my mother a few years before, she was shocked when I told her I was now a believer. But she quickly recovered and immediately made an appointment for me to meet with her minister. He received me in his office and listened carefully as I described my new faith.

"I love Jesus, but I don't know what to do next."

To my surprise, this old-time preacher did not suggest I go to church. Rather, he gave me a quick study on the reliability of the New Testament accounts of Jesus.

"The Gospels are historical documents based on eyewitness testimonies."

I said, "That's what the book of John seemed like to me."

"The Gospels were copied and distributed to many groups of Christians. But even though no originals remain, the variations found amongst the ancient copies are amazingly small."

"I didn't know that. That's amazing."

"The answers you are looking for, my young friend, will be found in the Bible."

THAT DECEMBER I PACKED MY bags and flew up to Austin. My two friends, David and Harvey, met me at the airport. I was startled because they no longer had shoulder length hair. But as we loaded my bags into their car, they laughed and ripped off their short hair wigs. They both had part-time jobs and needed to wear the wigs for cover. (Hmm. Maybe Austin wasn't as hip as I thought.) Anyway, we planned to share an apartment so our parental allowances would go further.

Harvey was working on an art degree. He was an easy-going guy, really chilled out. I don't know how he and David teamed up because David was kind of intense and enrolled in lots of business classes. He took advantage of the sex, drugs and rock and roll; but his long-term plan was to make a bundle of money. David had a girlfriend named Barbara who hung out with us on most weekends. She was quite the blond bombshell and I often puzzled over how David, a skinny dude like me, could have bagged her. When Barbara got stoned, she had the distracting habit of taking off her top. Since she never wore a bra, conversations were difficult. I kept losing my train of thought.

Now David thought himself quite a clever fellow and would have nothing to do with God or Jesus. But we were old pals and he was friendly even in his scorn for my new faith. Harvey was a different story. We had long discussions about the meaning of life and how God fit into the picture. I was still doing drugs—it was a hard habit to break—but I didn't feel good about it. Meanwhile, I took long walks to be alone with God, praying my simple prayers, and delighting in the knowledge that he loved me. David and Harvey got used to it.

While on one of these walks, I noticed the "Loony Bus" was back in town. This time I decided to talk to them and see what was going on. As I neared the bus I saw several people my age sitting around talking. A couple of them with guitars played what sounded like folk songs. A longhaired girl, wearing an ankle length granny dress and a blue jean jacket, stood behind a folding table piled with sandwiches and doughnuts.

"Are you hungry?" she asked. "How about a sandwich?"

"Uh, no thanks." (I wasn't in the habit of taking food from strangers, even pretty ones.)

"Then how about we go in the bus and rap?"

Back then "rapping" meant talking, not music. I didn't see any harm in stepping inside the bus to chat. And she was a rather attractive young lady. She told me her name was Hephzibah. Hephzibah? What kind of name was that? But she took my hand and steered me to the bus door. I saw it was just an old converted school bus. Most the seats were replaced with wooden benches and red sackcloth covered the interior. (These guys had a thing for red sackcloth.)

We sat down and she asked me the usual questions: my name, if I went to college, what I was studying, and finally leading up to the big question.

"Do you believe in God?"

"I do."

"What do you think about Jesus?"

"Jesus!" I exclaimed, "I love Jesus!"

"So do we," she said with a big smile.

Then she gave me a tight hug. (O Happy Day!) Hephzibah told me how she joined "The Family." (They called themselves the Family? That was intriguing.) I noticed Hephzibah wore something familiar dangling from her necklace.

"What is that thing you have on your necklace? I saw you guys wearing big ones in the park last summer."

She was thrilled. "Oh, were you there? You saw the vigil? Pretty mind blowing, right? Anyway, what you saw were yokes."

That made no sense to me. Wasn't a yoke an old timey thing you put on an animal?

So I asked, "But why do you wear them? Does it mean something?"

"First of all it means I am yoked to Christ. Jesus said, 'Take my yoke upon you and learn of me.'"

"Yoked to Jesus? Does it mean he'll help carry our loads?"

"Right! You get it. And there's another reason we wear them. The Bible says the prophet Jeremiah wore a heavy yoke around his neck to warn Israel about God's judgment upon their sins. We wear yokes because we believe judgment is coming to America unless it repents."

"Oh, I see." (Actually, I never heard of Jeremiah, so I was clueless.)

Hephzibah glanced out the window. "Hold on! There's someone you need to meet."

She darted off and returned with a guy wearing a guitar strapped to his back. He was a radiant fellow with long black hair, a thick mustache, and a beaming smile. He looked a few years older than me—I had just turned 18—and wore a pouch slung across his chest. It looked like something Davey Crocket might wear, not feminine. I thought, *Wow, I wonder what he's got in there?*

Hephzibah did the intros. "This is Cephas." He reached out and gave me the hippie handshake—so much cooler than the one our parents taught us. Then he sat down for a heart to heart.

"Hephzibah tells me you love Jesus."

"I do, I really do."

"Do you read the Bible?" Cephas asked.

"I try to, but some of it is hard to understand. I do like the book of John."

"Then let me show you something out of the book of John."

11

He reached into his pouch and pulled out a Bible (mystery solved). As he flipped through the pages, I saw words underlined and handwritten notes in the margins. Writing in a Bible? That was new to me.

Cephas pointed to a verse and said, "Jesus told everyone, 'Repent! For the Kingdom of Heaven has come.' You know what repent means? It means to change your mind. Jesus meant you need a revolution in your life to change the way you think and act!"

"I need to change. I've done some bad shit."

Cephas looked into my eyes. "We all do things we are ashamed of. Things we wish we could change. We blow it—that's what sin is—and the Bible says sin must be punished. But here's the good news: Jesus sacrificed his life so our sins could be forgiven."

I looked down. "I do need forgiveness."

Cephas said, "If you receive Jesus, you'll get it. You will become a child of God."

I asked, "Receive Jesus? How do you do that?"

"You just ask him to come into your heart and then you will be born again."

Born again? Ask him into your heart? These were unfamiliar terms to me. Cephas saw my puzzled look and found another verse.

"Jesus said, except a man be born again he shall not enter into the kingdom of heaven."

Hephzibah chimed in, "When you receive Jesus, it's like he plants a seed into your heart and a new person is born."

I still didn't see the difference between believing in Jesus and receiving him. But what did I know? Then Cephas closed the deal.

"Jesus is knocking at the door of your heart. He wants to come in and be with you forever. But you need to open the door and ask him in. All you have to do is pray. How about right now?"

We held hands and Cephas told me to say this prayer, "Jesus, I know I'm a sinner. I believe you died for me. Please come into my heart and let me be born again. Thank you for forgiving my sins."

When I repeated the prayer, Hephzibah and Cephas lifted their hands into the air and rejoiced. *Thank you, Lord. Praise you, Jesus. Hallelujah!* This went on for some time.

Then Cephas, with tears in his eyes, said, "You are now my true brother in Christ. Your life will never be the same."

He grabbed me, hugged me and kissed me on the neck. Kissed me on the neck? It never dawned on me to take it any other way than as an expression of deep affection. And I soaked it in like a dry sponge. Then someone called out for Cephas. As he trotted off, he said, "I hope I will see you again."

When we were alone, Hephzibah said, "Come back tomorrow at noon and you can have lunch with us. I'm glad you got to meet Cephas. He's a heavy brother."

I thought, heavy indeed. I was ripe, low-hanging fruit, ready to be plucked.

WHEN I RETURNED HOME, DAVID was out with Barbara.

But when I told Harvey about my encounter at the "Loony Bus," he was blown away. I told him I was going back the next day and he decided to come with me. We arrived around noon to find the bus empty except for a longhaired guy with a huge beard sitting in the driver's seat. He told us everyone was at the park.

He added, "If you get over there quick, you'll be in time to see the Holy Ghost Sample."

Holy Ghost Sample? What in the world was that? We made our way to the park in time to see about 15 Family members standing around in a large clearing. Cephas was there, tuning his guitar with a few other musicians. When he noticed me coming, he stepped away and greeting us warmly with hugs all round (big huggers, these guys).

Cephas said, "You guys are just in time to hear us play."

Time for a Holy Ghost Sample

All the family members, including the musicians, formed a large circle and encouraged Harvey and me to join them. The guitar players strummed and we all clapped in time with the music. This got the attention of other folks in the park who strolled over to see the action. Then the musicians sang their songs, mostly about Jesus. As things got ramped up, girls with tambourines danced around to the music. It wasn't like what you would see kids do on *American Bandstand*, just some hopping around, leg kicking and arm swaying. Still, it was a pleasant sight. This went on for a few more songs. Then everyone in the circle sat down. By then a fairly large crowd had gathered.

One of the musicians said in a loud friendly voice, "If anyone is hungry we'd like to invite you to have lunch with us. But first, we're going to put on a little skit for you."

As he played his guitar, he sang some lines to a simple tune, like he was the narrator of a play.

"There once was a boy named Randy. In the morning he was feeling dandy."

At those words another guy from the Family jumped into the middle of the circle and strutted around, obviously feeling dandy.

"Randy had himself a new car. And he drove it near and far."

The Randy guy held an imaginary steering wheel and pretended to drive around while making Vroom-Vroom noises.

"Randy had a pretty girly. Everyone called her Shirley."

Then Randy looked around in the crowd and invited a hippie chick to join him in the circle. She refused with a laugh. But the next girl he invited was a good sport and came in with Randy, receiving a hand from the audience.

"They jumped in Randy's car. And drove to a disco bar."

After more pretend driving, they screeched to a halt and acted out going into the disco bar to order drinks.

"Randy's girl was getting bored. So he took her out on the dance floor."

As the couple started dancing, the guy playing Randy pretended to be an outlandish dancer. This produced huge laughs from the audience.

Okay, so you get the picture. As the skit proceeded, Randy lost the girl, lost his money, lost his car, and wound up disgusted with his life.

Some of the skit participants were Family members and others were plucked from the audience. There were lots of laughs and claps from the gathered crowd. The finale of the skit came when another Family member entered and told Randy, who was no longer feeling dandy, that the answer to his problems was Jesus. Several Bible verses later, Randy asked Jesus into his heart. Everything was dandy again, including eternal life.

After one more song, the Family members dispersed into the crowd to talk one-on-one with the observers. Lunch was set up on some blankets nearby and some folks made their way over to the food. Then Cephas and Hephzibah approached us. Hephzibah focused her attention on Harvey while Cephas and I sat down under a tree.

This time Cephas listened as I told him what was going on in my head and heart. As I bared my soul, I felt Cephas understood where I was coming from. In short, he got me. He was interested in me. Then he told me his story:

"My wife and I were struggling with life. We were both surfers and one day we met some Christians on the beach who persuaded us to give our lives to Jesus. We went to their house and never left. Jesus told his disciples to give up everything to follow him. But He promised they would get back much more. My wife and I left our old lives behind, but we got a new life and a real family."

Harvey left shortly after lunch, but Cephas and I spoke until early evening. He often pulled out his well-worn Bible and read verses to confirm the things he was saying. The way he flipped through and found verses was like a magician doing fancy card flourishes. He showed me a verse from the book of Acts where it said all the believers were together and had all things in common. They even sold their possessions and distributed them to whoever had need.

"See? We live in colonies with other Christians just like they did in the early church."

Cephas really knew his Bible and I was mightily impressed. But more than that, his words were like sparks and started a blaze in my heart. I longed for such a life with a real family and a real purpose. I wanted more than anything to give my life to Jesus and serve him faithfully.

Cephas, and his wife Shiloh

Cephas said, "I know deep in your heart you love Jesus just like I do. I think Jesus is saying to you, right now, 'Come and follow me.' Do you want to be a disciple and serve the Lord?"

I was almost in tears, "Yes! Yes I do."

Cephas put his hands on my shoulders, shut his eyes and began praising the Lord for my deliverance from the bondage of the world.

"We are leaving on the bus in the morning. Come back with all your possessions, brother, and your new life will begin."

During my long walk back to the apartment, I was thinking, "*Should* I do it? *Can* I do it? Nah! There's *no way* I can do it."

I decided to do it.

Back at the apartment David was still nowhere to be found. Harvey was dumbstruck when I told him my plan. He didn't try talking me out of it—David would have. I think Harvey recognized the fire within me would be hard to extinguish.

After talking for hours Harvey said, "I hope this makes you happy, but I don't understand it. I wish I did."

2

"I can't stand the water!" cried the Gingerbread Man
Said the fox, "I will take you across to the land
If you hop on my tail you'll have nothing to fear
High and dry on my back you will be safe, my dear"

BABY BOOMER ONBOARD

AT THE CRACK OF DAWN, I took the long walk back to the bus. Cephas and Hephzibah greeted me with jubilation. I was now a family member, a brother. This was really happening. I was giving up my life for Jesus. It was January 24, 1971. After the group loaded onto the bus, we hit the road. About a dozen or so brothers and sisters made up the team, including the two new disciples: me and one other guy.

I went along for the ride.

I noticed all the men had these funny little pouches slung on the shoulders containing their Bibles, tracts and (without fail) a toothbrush. The women carried their stuff in larger purses.

One interesting guy named David Z. stood out from the rest. I'm not sure what the Z stood for (maybe Zest or Zeal); but he was quite a character—a ball of fire. His eyes glowed with excitement and his smile implied secret knowledge. "Mercurial" is the word that comes to mind. Apart from Cephas, David Z. appeared to be one of the leaders.

Lots of praying went on as we traveled. I noticed prayers were always addressed to "Lord-Father-God." It was always *Lord-Father-God this* and *Lord-Father-God that*. And here's another thing, during prayers I would hear them launch into words that sounded like a foreign language. What did I think? *Wow! They must be quoting Bible verses in the original Hebrew or Greek.* I was really impressed.

But when I asked David Z. about it, he chuckled and said. "No, we are speaking in tongues. Haven't you been baptized in the Holy Spirit?"

I knew nothing about speaking in tongues (or even the Holy Spirit for that matter). Swish! David Z's Bible was whipped out and I got a quick lesson on the necessity of a "second blessing" after you got saved. Holy Spirit baptism gave you the power to serve God. Verses in the book of Acts described people receiving the Holy Spirit and speaking in tongues.

David Z. said, "'Tongues' is a gift you might receive. It's like angel's language."

When he told the group I needed the Holy Spirit, everyone surrounded me, laid their hands on me, and prayed earnestly for the Spirit to come upon me. I joined in the great rejoicing that followed, even though I felt quite the same as before.

Cephas said, "Our next destination is Houston. We'll hit all the parks and go witnessing."

"Witnessing? What's that?"

I soon found out it meant going around and telling other people about Jesus. When we got to a park, we would pile out of the bus and preach to anyone who would listen. It was very much like what I had seen at the park in Austin: free food was offered, songs were sung, skits were performed, and testimonies were given. As a novice, I just tagged along with one of the brothers to watch them in action. Now and then they would refer to me as a new disciple who had heard the call. I did see several young people who were receptive and prayed to receive Jesus. But nobody dropped everything and rode off with us on the bus.

Going on the road was a thrilling way to start my new life. Sometimes we had a house to sleep in. Sometimes we all slept in the bus. Singing, swapping stories, sharing whatever food we had—it was my own personal Woodstock. All this and Jesus, too! After several days we headed back to "base" camp (the main Texas colony).

Before we left town, I decided to call my mom from a payphone. I didn't dare call my father because I knew he would go berserk. As I've said, my mother was a Christian and—get this—I actually thought she would be happy for me. That's where I was wrong. When I told her my "good news" on the phone, she got very upset. I told her I was now following Jesus, but it didn't help. Her rejection stunned me. After she hung up I broke down in tears.

But really, what did I expect?

Hey Mom, I just dropped out of school and I'm travelling with a gypsy band of Jesus freaks. What? You're not happy about it?

Cephas told me I should not be discouraged because even Christ's family didn't understand him. In fact, they thought Jesus was out of his mind. Then David Z. showed me a verse where Jesus told his followers to expect opposition from their own families—"A man's foes shall be they of his own household."

David Z. clapped me on the back and said, "Brother, you just had your first challenge. Praise God, you passed the test."

It took me a while to get over my mother's negative reaction. But it was a comforting thought. *Hmm… even Jesus got flak from his family.* And besides, didn't I have a new family now?

Lots of singing and praising the Lord happened on the bus.

This was known as "having inspiration." During these sessions, people took turns sharing the stories of their past lives, especially how they came to Jesus and joined the Family. This practice was called "giving your testimony." As I listened to each story, I could relate. We had something in common—something that inclined us to drop out of the establishment.

As we traveled further and further north, it felt like my old life was passing away. And that's what I hoped for—to leave my past behind. Not that I had it so hard as a kid. I grew up in the suburbs during the fifties and sixties where we all survived the dangers of cars without seatbelts, riding our bikes and skateboards without helmets, and roaming our neighborhoods until late at night without being kidnapped.

My family was very, very middle class. Our small Houston home was in a neighborhood next to a big pine forest with paths to explore and creeks to splash in. All the kids in the neighborhood spent most of their free time outdoors. It's popular today for people to bemoan the fact that children spend too much time on computers or phones and not enough time playing outside. We did have a blast back in those days, but I don't think it did much to advance our moral development. Kids can be little shits whether indoors or out. I was a free-range little shit.

My sister was three years older than me. She might tell a different story, but as for me, I think we mostly got along. Apart from the occasional spankings we received—and justly deserved—our parents did not mistreat us. However, we were both aware that my father had quite a temper. This was amply demonstrated whenever we were all together in the car. Dad was easily irritated by other drivers and would frequently let loose with a string of foul language and social commentary, especially if the offending driver was female or Mexican. I always preferred riding in the back compartment of our station wagon as far from the driver's seat as possible. My sister and I learned many techniques to avoid my father's wrath in the car: don't poke the back of his seat with your feet or chew on ice or smack your gum and so on. But even so, road trips were never a pleasant experience.

At home I treaded lightly around my father. Although it was a stressful situation that certainly soured our father-son relationship, I wouldn't call it abuse. Actually, my dad was the one with the rotten childhood. After his mother died, his father abandoned him in East Texas when he was just three years old. Eventually a man and his wife took in my dad as extra labor on their small dirt farm. They did raise him, but he was never treated as one of their kin. When they had family over for dinner, my father ate separately in the kitchen. After years of living like a servant, Dad escaped a hard life of poverty and enlisted in the army as soon as he was able. After World War Two, he went to law school on the GI Bill. After graduating, he set up shop in Tyler, Texas. That's where he met my mother.

My mother's parents disliked my father from the start. They were devout members of the Church of Christ and recognized a heathen when they saw one (even though my father feigned interest in the church while seducing my mother). I'm sure my mother looked upon my father as a project—someone she could convert. I don't think they would have married, except my mother got pregnant with my sister. After the shotgun wedding, my father moved my mother as far as he could get from her parents. Nevertheless, my mother's religious upbringing followed doggedly. She constantly nagged my father about his drinking, even to the point of pouring out his booze and locking him out of the house when he came home drunk. It ended one night with a busted down door.

My mother declared, "I never want to see liquor in the house again."

My father responded, "In that case, don't ever ask me where I have been when I don't come home."

My mother and father stayed unhappily married for 17 years. Perhaps as penance for her indiscretions with my father, my mother decided to double down on her religion. This caused many cracks in the marital relationship. My father, who did what he thought was right by marrying my mother after knocking her up, had no interest in the church or anything that might interfere with his vices. I could feel the tension between my parents and, as a result, I spent lots of time at my friends' houses. When I had to be home, I played by myself in my room. It was like my fantasy hideaway. Reading was my constant escape. One of my favorite books was *Pippi Longstocking* because Pippi lived alone, except for her monkey and horse, with no parents. That seemed like a wonderful thing. I often daydreamed about running away from home.

I was not the son my father expected. He was a big man who loved sports and was an avid hunter. But unlike my dad, I was rather small-boned and not proficient in any sport. The sports events I attended and the teams I was encouraged to join were a source of torture for me. No doubt this was a disappointment for my father, but he didn't give up—there was always hunting. Though I tried hiding it, I loathed hunting. When each season approached, I was filled with dread. One time I shot a bird and went to pick it up. It was still alive, staring at me in shock, with a wounded wing. I took it back to my father and asked if we could repair the damage. As we inspected the bird's bloody wing, I fainted.

I know my father loved me in his own puzzled way. But what to do with me? That was the challenge for him because our passions and interests divided us. Deep inside I longed for a father figure in my life; but the older I got, the less my father and I spoke. When I first saw the movie *To Sir With Love*, I cried because I needed a Sidney Poitier, someone wise to guide me. Poor dad... he wanted an Esau, but my mother gave him a Jacob.

My sister and I were hauled to church every Sunday morning and evening and again on Wednesday night. We were also shuffled off during the summer weeks to vacation bible school. We also attended Sunday school before each Sunday sermon. When past nursery age, children were expected to sit still through the sermons. I did gain a couple of advantages from the services. I became an expert in tying and untying knots in the long hymnal ribbons. I also developed an aptitude for drawing cartoon figures on the contribution envelopes placed in little wooden racks on the back of each pew. These two talents served me well in my adult life. When those pursuits bored me, I would entertain myself by crossing my legs until one of them fell asleep, then uncrossing them and enjoying the transition from numbness to pins and needles. That pretty much sums up my early religious training. Apart from boredom, I really have nothing to complain about—no scars on my psyche by twisted priests like you read about in Stephen King novels.

As far as sex education, I asked my mother what the "F word" meant after hearing it from the boys in my Cub Scout pack. Appropriately outraged, she instructed me to never repeat it. But it did provide an opportunity for *THE TALK* ("when two people love each other, the man plants a seed inside the woman, etc."). This didn't clear things up very much. Previously—a standard practice in those days—I had been stuck in a bathtub with my younger female cousin. I couldn't recall seeing any place where I could plant anything (the belly button was my best guess). And where did I get these magic seeds from, anyway? Not to worry... it wasn't long before I got a more detailed picture from our preacher's son. One afternoon my mother dragged me along to visit the pastor's wife. While the adults were busy chatting, the preacher's kid took me into his room and introduced me to my first Playboy magazine—an unexpected bonus. He didn't fill in all the blanks concerning reproduction, but I gained a clearer picture—the boy's thing fits into the girl's thing.

My mother regularly took me to the library to check out books. One afternoon I discovered a special volume—*The Illustrated Book of Magic Tricks*. I sucked up the contents of that book like mother's milk and immediately scrounged around for the necessary paraphernalia: cards, coins, handkerchiefs and candles. You would never see such a book these days because some of the tricks were marked with a skull and crossbones picture to indicate they were dangerous. Of course, I had to learn those tricks first. As soon as I had practiced and fooled my mother with several feats of prestidigitation, I put together a show for my Cub Scout troop. It was a great success and launched me in a hobby that filled my childhood and teenage years.

When I finished elementary school, our family moved from Houston to the Rio Grande Valley. Once there, we saw less and less of my father (which was a relief). But I have rather unpleasant memories of that time because I was a late bloomer. At age thirteen I looked like I belonged in elementary school. That certainly made my junior high experience special. All the other boys were beefing up and growing hair in unexpected places. All the girls were at least a foot taller than me. I was definitely not a part of the in-crowd. And of course, just to make those golden years complete, there were the mandatory bullies. It was the only time in my life when I had fantasies of committing murder.

The mystery of my father's absence from the home cleared up a few years later when my sister (then seventeen) eloped with her boyfriend to get married in Mexico. My mother—desperate to find my father—was eventually given a possible location. It turned out to be my sneaky dad's second home where he and his mistress were enjoying each other's company. In a rage my mother slapped *the other woman* in the face, knocked over some furniture, and dragged my father out. She told him she would forgive him if he stopped the extra-marital relationship. Her offer being refused, my mother carted me off back to Houston.

My father told me later the only reason he stayed with my mother so long was for the benefit of his children. I may be wrong, but I think an earlier break would have been better for everyone. As my mother and father grew further apart, I likewise emotionally distanced myself from them both. The divorce finally destroyed any pretense of a family.

In the days following, I endured my mother's moral outrage as she spewed forth her spite and bitterness. She was the one wronged and my father was the adulterer. We camped out in my aunt's spare room for months while Mom searched for a house. It was a rough patch for both of us, especially since puberty had finally begun raging through my body.

After the mess my sister made, my mother thought I would be the good one. Alas, that was not to be. My mother immediately found a new church and, at first, I attended services with her regularly. But eventually I announced I was done with church.

My mother sputtered, "If you want to live in my house, you will have to attend."

"Okay, Mom, I'll go live with my father."

Thus we reached a stalemate—mutually assured destruction. I was released from the church requirement and found myself pretty much in charge of my own moral training.

I entered high school thinking I was in for four more years of the same old crap. I wanted to fit in, but felt inferior, like such an oddball. I wanted my life to change, to get better, but no matter how hard I tried, it seemed like I was stuck with being me. I wrote this poem when I was fifteen years old:

My will is weak
In vain I seek
A stone to step on
A crutch to lean on
But I have found none

I did have one thing up my sleeve that made me stand out in high school—my magic tricks. So I signed up to perform my act during a school talent show. Soon everyone around the campus called me the "Magic Man." Unfortunately, it put me in the nerd category instead of the "Cool Dude" status I craved. When I figured this out, I took my conjuring passion underground and just performed at children's birthday parties for extra cash.

Most days my mother was at work when I got home from school. Our next-door neighbor was an older man who was courting my mother. My first exposure to alcohol involved sneaking into his house when he was out to take swigs from his well-stocked liquor cabinet. It was clear to me people didn't drink the stuff for the taste—I held my nose to get it down—but the buzz was quite a revelation. Here was a liquid to make you happy… at least for a while.

And then came those high school assemblies where they warned us about the dangers of mind-altering drugs. Those meetings had the opposite effect on me. I left them wondering where I could get some of these drugs. I was quite ready to jump on the freak wagon. Why not? I already thought I was a freak. I wanted to alter my identity and my feelings about myself. And wham! Doing drugs accomplished both. And at long last I found myself part of a group—the anti-establishment doper community.

By the tenth grade I had an efficient way to deal with my sentence on Devil's Island, also known as public high school: chugging booze and smoking dope. Inevitably, I added LSD, Peyote, Speed and Cocaine into my drug cocktail. Whenever I could drum up the cash, I got stoned. How I managed to graduate from high school remains a mystery.

You know, people always say cult members are brainwashed; but my brain was pre-washed by the hippy counter-culture. I was a card-carrying member of the psychedelic sixties, already marching to the drop-out drumbeat. The cult not only exploited my dysfunctional family background, but also my rebellious attitude. My rickety infrastructure made it easy to hear stuff like, "Your parents don't have the truth. But you, you're a real truth seeker. Join our revolution for Jesus and we can change the world."

When I finally did move up to Austin, I was looking for answers. And then came my fateful encounter with the Children of God. And here I was on the Loony Bus, riding high on the fervor of my radical decision. I had no doubts. I was following Jesus. This would be great!

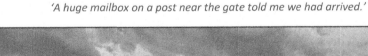

AFTER A LONG BUS RIDE, we arrived at the base colony.

It was called "The Texas Soul Clinic," but everyone on the bus just used the initials (TSC). It was located near the very small town of Mingus, about an hour and a half west of Dallas. I don't recall seeing any town as we neared our destination, just miles and miles of two-lane highways. We finally turned onto a dirt road that led up to an entrance gate like the ones I used to open for my grandfather when he took me to feed his cows. The fences near the gate displayed big wooden signs with Bible verses. A huge mailbox on a post near the gate told me we had arrived.

'A huge mailbox on a post near the gate told me we had arrived.'

The bus driver honked a few times and someone came and let us in.

We rolled onto the property, past several smaller structures, until we finally came to a large dining hall. When we piled out of the bus, dozens of young folks surrounded me. They were mostly my age—kids really— all happy, smiling and quick to give you a hug. A bus arrival was a big deal at TSC.

'A bus arrival was a big deal at TSC.'

After our enthusiastic reception, we were given something to drink and a snack. I can't remember what they served, but odds are we got peanut butter sandwiches. By the time we were done, it was getting dark outside. Cephas fetched a flashlight and led his two new converts along a well-trodden path.

"Where are we going?" I asked.

Cephas called out, "To the Babes' Ranch!"

I wondered, "What in the world is a Babes' Ranch?"

In Neverland you'll find that life is very good
All the children live together deep in the wood
We will teach you how to love some serious play
But watch out for pirates who might steal you away

BABES' RANCH

EARLY THE NEXT MORNING I woke up in a crowded dorm room. Bunk beds were crammed throughout several connecting rooms, looking a bit like those prison scenes you see in movies. I lay there for a while, trying to orient myself to my new reality. After I got dressed, I wondered what was next.

It wasn't long before a guy named Joab walked into the room. He was the Babe's Ranch shepherd in charge of all the new converts. (Just so you know, in the Family all leaders were called shepherds.)

I remember Joab's friendly eyes and warm smile as he invited me and the other new guy into this little trailer near the bunkhouse. I guess it was like his office.

"Welcome to the Babes' Ranch," he said.

Still curious, I asked, "Why is it called a *Babes' Ranch*?"

"Well, the Bible says new disciples are *babes in Christ*. You two are the babies of the Family. Before you start your basic classes, we must take care of a few things. The first order of business is to discuss this important document: ***The Revolutionary Sheet***."

He handed us mimeographed pages and said, "We can read this together. If you have any questions, don't be afraid to stop me. It's cool. After all, you need to know what you're getting into."

Joab was quite the talker, often going off on rabbit trails and tossing in his own stories about the Family. It was a long presentation, but to me, very engaging. The paper listed all the requirements for membership. It also covered the group's basic beliefs. Scattered through the document were lots (and I mean lots) of Bible references in shorthand (like Jn. 3:16). And Joab didn't skip a single one. He stopped at each reference, flipped through his Bible, and read the verse for us.

Joab giving a class

I've constructed an abridged version of that document, minus the Bible verses, to give you some insight into what it was like in those early days. (Later, most of the rules were discarded and replaced with new ones—just like the pigs did with the commandments written on the barn wall in George Orwell's *Animal Farm*.)

- You must study and learn the beliefs found in our revolutionary handbook: the Bible.
- You must be in good health because the life of the revolutionary is rigorous.
- You must be at least 16 years old or have parental consent.
- You must be free of debts and legal obligations.
- You must attend all classes and meetings.

- No smoking or drugs are allowed.
- No dating is allowed. No smooching! Marriage is mainly for leadership.
- You are expected to obey leadership without question.
- You must perform all duties without complaint.
- Your living quarters must be kept tidy and your body clean.
- You must obey all the laws of the land (unless a law is against a command of God).
- Personal possessions are limited to a small suitcase, 2-3 inches of hang-up clothing, a coat, bedroll, Bible, writing materials and a musical instrument.
- New disciples can be searched for anything not allowed in colonies. Also, leadership can read all incoming and outgoing mail.
- Disciples are not allowed to leave the colony without permission.
- We believe in the Father, the Son and the Holy Spirit.
- We believe once you accept Jesus Christ as your savior, you will be saved. And once you get saved, you will always be saved. You can never lose your salvation.
- Doing good works WILL NOT save you; but good works WILL give you rewards in heaven.
- We believe in the baptism of the Holy Spirit, which gives you the power to witness. You might also receive spiritual gifts, like prophecy, teaching, healing or speaking in tongues.
- We are following the radical pattern of Christ and His disciples. We reject all mainline denominations as corrupt.
- Full-time discipleship is the best way to serve the Lord. We give up our old lives and live together communally with other Christians so we can dedicate ourselves to prayer, Bible study and preaching the Gospel to the whole world.

I didn't make up the "no smooching" part; it really was in there. That cracked me up because the last time I came across smooching was in the *Archie* comic books I used to read. But I had no difficulty with anything I read on the Revolutionary Sheet. In fact, after going over all the verses I was more convinced than ever I was on solid ground. Not so with the other new guy. He had a problem with the rule about mail being opened by leadership.

He said, "What's the reason for that? Isn't anything private?"

I remember my feeling: *Hey, this guy just doesn't get it. This is radical. Our lives are changed. The leaders would only require such a thing for our protection.*

Joab was not fazed by this guy's reaction. "We are in God's army. Our enemy, the devil, will temp us to leave the good fight. He will try using our old friends and families to tempt us away from the good fight. But listen, nobody's forcing you to do anything. If you have a problem, you are free to leave. There's a bus stop right down the road. However, if you want to serve the Lord and be a part of this revolution, just sign at the bottom."

In the end, we both signed up. Then Joab moved on to the next step.

"To be a disciple you have to give up all your possessions. From now on, any funds or gifts you receive from your parents will be distributed to wherever the need is greatest."

Cephas had already prepped me for what he called *forsaking all*. He told me how he and his wife gave up all they owned. So I was ready. Actually, it was no big deal since all I had was a backpack full of clothes, a bit of cash, and a suitcase filled with odds and ends. The hardest thing I gave up was my precious *Jesus Christ: Superstar album*. (I never told anyone, but I hid a paperback book at the bottom of my backpack—*The Essential Lenny Bruce*. It would be a few months before I finally parted with that.)

Joab gave us time to sort through our gear and set aside the items we could keep (as listed on The Revolutionary Sheet.) We took what was left to a small building to drop off the rest. A sign on the door read **"The Free Store."** Family members could visit the store if they needed anything—a shirt or a pair of pants or whatever.

The next item of business took it further—we had to give up our old names as a symbol of our new lives. Joab said it was customary to pick a name from the Bible. I had been thinking of changing my name to James, but Joab said it was already taken. He handed me a list of Bible names up for grabs. I scanned it and thought, *"Buz? Dodo? Man, some of these names are really weird."* Then I came across SALEM.

I asked, "What about Salem? Who was he?"

Joab said, "Salem is a place, not a person. Salem means *peace*. It's an ancient name for Jerusalem—city of PEACE—get it?"

And just like that, the old me was gone. I was born again as Salem, a new creature.

Our final task—and the hardest—was writing back home so our parents would know where we were. I wrote three letters: one to my mother, one to my father, and one to my sister. I whipped off the letter to my father first and made it short since I knew it wouldn't make any difference what I wrote to him. But I was close to my sister and my letter to her was more emotional. I told her what was going on and how I knew that she, of all my family members, might understand why I took such a radical step. I also pleaded with her to consider following Jesus herself and included several Bible verses. Last on the list was my mother. I actually have that letter because after my mother's death I discovered a shoebox where she kept everything I had ever written to her (from childhood on up).

> Dear Mother,
>
> As I told you on the phone, a wonderful thing has changed my life. You knew I was searching for answers. After I talked to your minister, I started reading the New Testament. I read the verse where it says, "Seek and ye shall find." So, I prayed to find the truth and now I have it. In Austin I came across the Christian group known as the Children of God. When I saw the love in their eyes, and how they totally devoted their lives to spreading the word of God, I knew it was what I was looking for. So far it's been more than I ever dreamed. The group reaches many young people and takes confused kids off the streets and off dope. I will write you again often. If you want to write me, address the letter to Salem. That is my new Bible name. God Bless You!

Letters written, Joab took us on a tour of the whole property. It reminded me of the cowboy movies Clint Eastwood made—you know, the Spaghetti Westerns.

Starting at the front gate, we walked along a dirt road and came to several little buildings that looked like those motel rooms you pass on the highway. Most of these were used as bunkhouses, some for the sisters and others for the brothers. Another building served as a little school for the Family's children.

Two brothers make their way to the Dining Hall

Then we came to the main kitchen and dining hall. Behind this was a pleasant little pond surrounded by short trees. A stone's throw away was a print shop. Parked around the property were several small trailers for married couples—the leaders.

Finally we headed back to the Babes' Ranch and were given time to settle in. Joab said we would stay at the Babes' Ranch for about three months. Our time would be filled with Bible classes and duties around the TSC ranch, like washing dishes, working in the laundry, helping with food prep or joining work parties to clean up the buildings or grounds.

We knew it was time for dinner when someone banged on a large triangle outside the kitchen. We saw groups of people walking towards the dining hall from different directions. Once inside, I joined about a hundred brothers and sisters seated at several very long tables that were crammed into the space. At one end of the hall I saw a small raised platform with a microphone and speaker set up. At the other end was the entrance to the kitchen. The food was dished out on metal plates. As you can imagine, it was loud in there with everyone talking at the same time.

At one point a bearded fellow named *Zach the Greek* came out of the kitchen wearing an apron. He got our attention by banging on a metal trash can with an industrial size spoon. Then he yelled, "Scrape your plates!" Except this guy spoke with a pretty heavy accent so it sounded more like "Screpa you pletas!" This got an immediate response from the entire dining hall as everyone shouted back at him, "SCREPA YOU PLETAS!" It seemed like this was a mealtime ritual.

After eating, we dutifully scraped our plates and placed them in a huge tub of hot soapy water. When things were settled down, brothers and sisters mounted the platform with guitars and played some Family songs. I had never heard anything like those songs in church (or anywhere else for that matter). The audience clapped and sang along. Some people even got up and danced in the spirit. After each song ended, you could expect an explosion as people lifted up their hands and praised God.

David Z. was up on the platform and frequently shouted, "REVOLUTION!" Then the whole crowd held up their hands with three fingers stretched out and shouted back in response, "FOR JESUS!" (Three fingers for Father, Son and Holy Spirit.) Then he would scream, "HOLY

GHOST!" And everyone held up one fist and yelled back, "POWER!"

Later, someone named Jethro came into the hall and stood on the platform. He looked kind of thirtyish to me—older than most of the others at TSC. Besides that, he had short hair and dressed like my father. But the group greeted him with enthusiasm and affection. Jethro called upon members of the bus team to mount the stage and give testimonies. Cephas and David Z. gave an exciting rendition of the bus travels, the Holy Ghost Samples, the number of people who received Jesus, the way the Lord supplied food and places to stay, and the new members who joined. Eventually, I was tugged up on the stage where I gave my halting, wide-eyed testimony. Lots more praising and hugging followed. What a day! When the meeting ended, I was exhausted and happy to head over to my little bunk bed. I slept like a baby (or, I should say, a babe).

A FEW DAYS LATER I awoke with some abdominal distress.

When I told Joab about it, he took me to see Shadrack—a brother who acted as a kind of wild-west doctor for the group. He had been an army medic in Vietnam and knew some basic stuff.

He asked, "What's the trouble, brother?"

"I don't know. I just have this painful pressure."

"How long since you took a shit?"

"Not since I came to TSC."

When Shadrack heard this, he took me to the kitchen and gave me some water with a measure of Epsom Salt mixed in.

"This will fix you right up."

I drank it down obediently, not knowing what to expect. After a minute it felt like an alien would pop out of my intestines. I fell to my knees overwhelmed by the distress. Two of the cooks rushed over, laid hands on me, and prayed for my relief. Then Shadrack supported me as we did a fast trot to the nearest outhouse. (If you don't know what an outhouse is, look it up.) I barely made it in time. After hearing the explosion, Shadrack popped his head in and gave me a wink.

"Works every time," he said.

Eventually I reached for the toilet paper and saw a sign on the wall—*Revolutionaries use three sheets*. Hold on… just three little sheets of toilet paper? Now that would take a genuine ass-wiping miracle. I tried it and failed miserably. But since I had saved up my poop for several days, I was only slightly guilty about using more.

Apart from that incident, I had little trouble settling into my new routine. Reveille at seven in the morning was usually a guy who walked around with a guitar singing, *"Rise and shine and give God the glory."* After tending to our toilet and grooming needs, we headed off to do chores around the colony. Around mid-morning we had the first meal of the day (brunch). We ate a lot of oatmeal. Sometimes they served grains of wheat that were boiled until soft—a surprisingly good dish when seasoned with salt and margarine.

After chow, we returned to the Babe's Ranch for two or three Bible studies. We sat around wherever we could find a space. After classes, we were usually given a bit of free time—a precious unregimented slice of the day. But guess what? We usually spent it reading our Bibles or reviewing our verses. We couldn't get enough of it.

At the sound of that loud dinner bell, we made our way to the dining hall for the largest meal of the day. I can assure you, no food was wasted—we all cleaned our plates. We gobbled down foods we wouldn't have touched before joining the Family. (Liver? Yummy!) Since no one had a job, I wondered where all this food came from. But that was a mystery to be revealed at a future date.

At the end of the day everyone at TSC gathered together for "Inspiration." Just like on the bus, the guitars were whipped out and the air rang with lusty full-throated singing and clapping to the beat. After each song we closed our eyes and stretched out our arms to heaven with praises that went on for minutes. When we prayed together we were on our knees with our faces down on the ground. This was my first concept of worship and I absolutely loved it. It totally matched how I felt about God.

Those with musical ability were encouraged to write songs. I think you would be surprised at the number of beautiful songs composed by Family members. The ones I loved most were Bible verses put to music—

like Psalm 100 ("Make a joyful noise unto the Lord"). Apart from those, we also had songs about salvation ("Ya gotta be a baby to go to heaven"), testimonial songs ("I once was a lonely hippie; I had no place to go"), songs about the coming fall of America ("You better repent and get right with God") and songs celebrating our brotherly love and communal way of life ("How long have you been waiting for someone to love you?").

We danced to the lively tunes.

Musicians would often try out new songs during the nightly inspiration meetings. Some were great and went on to be added to the Family's musical catalog. Others fell flat. I remember a brother who got up and loudly sang, "The system is fucked and it's getting me down. Oh, Lord I can't stand it!" During the chorus he shot his middle finger into the air to show his scorn for the Devil's system. I knew that one wouldn't go far.

It made me very uncomfortable because I have never shot the finger at anyone. This is probably due to an experience I had in Sunday school when I was about five years old. To my kindergarten mind my middle finger looked like a cannon on wheels. So, I passed the time during the lesson imagining a battle raging between my two middle fingers. My mom, who happened to be the Sunday school teacher that week, walked over in shock and swatted my little fingers. It took me years to figure out why.

That's the only Family song I ever heard with the F-bomb—kind of wild, right? But tossing out expletives was commonplace at TSC. I think the leadership—most in their early twenties—thought using the language of the streets would make is easier to communicate with the hippie types we witnessed to. The same went for new converts, most of whom were former dopers. It didn't bother us to hear an exhortation like, "Satan is full of shit! Don't believe his lies!" It delivered a subtle message: *"We aren't like those strait-laced, self-righteous church folks. We are real, man. We are radical."* The leaders assured us, "There's nothing wrong with those good old Anglo-Saxon words. It's a hypocritical system that has declared them taboo. Just use wisdom and don't use that language when talking to your parents."

As a Lenny Bruce fan, I could dig it. His famous book was *How to Talk Dirty and Influence People.* He said, "Society gives these words power, especially if you use them in anger." However, let me be clear, the Children of God had limits when it came to crude language. You never ever heard any Family member take the Lord's name in vain. Things like "goddam" or "Oh my God!" were strictly forbidden.

Apart from salty language, the Family had its own set of shorthand speech. For example, we called the police "Romans." Church buildings were labeled "Temples of Baal" because they preached "churchianity" instead of what we considered truth. "Moloch" (a Canaanite god of child sacrifice) had two meanings in the Family: either the world's ungodly educational system or the practice of abortion. "Idols" were anything in your life you loved more than God, like possessions, people or pleasures. We thought "The Whore of Babylon" (found in the book of Revelation) was a symbol for America. Parents who gave disciples a hard time were called "ten-thirty-sixers," in reference to Matthew 10:36 (the verse Cephas quoted after my phone call to my mom). I could go on and on about this secret lingo, but I'm sure you get the general idea. (I'll toss in more as I move along.)

After our nightly meetings we usually had "quiet time" before lights out. Most nights we were own our own; but once a week we were required to write letters to our folks back home—this was a requirement. I suppose there were three main reasons for this. First, leadership didn't want parents freaking out and calling the police with claims we were being held against our will. Second, we were taught to give our former friends and family the message of salvation (along with warnings about God's future punishment for America if she didn't repent). Third, we always asked for financial support. Just to make it look official, we used writing papers with an impressive heading at the top.

Seriously, that was the formula for letters: (1) I'm very happy; so don't worry about me. (2) You need to get saved and repent before God unleashes His wrath. (3) And while you're at it, can you please send us some money? The last bit was called "spoiling Egypt." It was taken from a Bible story where the Israelites (also known as the Children of God, get it?) asked the Egyptians for gold and jewelry before the Exodus. Our parents were still stuck in "Egypt"—the worldly system we had escaped.

MOST OF MY TIME WAS filled with intense Bible studies.

Since this was our main source of indoctrination, I'll spend some time on what we studied. Our first classes covered topics like "Salvation," "Proof of Biblical Inspiration," "Creation VS Evolution," "The Message of Jeremiah: the Coming Fall of America," "Flesh or Spirit" and "Why the King James Bible Is the Only Inspired Version." I sat through lots of these beginner-level lessons. If I went into much detail about these classes, it would be tedious; but I think the titles give you the gist. With these out of the way, we were given classes on complete books of the Bible, starting with the book of Acts (since that was supposed to be our blueprint for communal living). For me, these lessons were very interesting and exciting—this was my first time ever to really study the Bible in depth.

Joab gave me a new hardback Bible (King James Version, of course) along with a small card listing memory verses. This was called "The Set Card" because it consisted of ten groups of verses that progressed from basic doctrine (the milk of the Word) to heavier stuff (the meat). At the bottom there were several whole Bible chapters to memorize. You could find copies of the Set Card posted on walls all over TSC. When I first saw the set card, it seemed like it would be a daunting task to master all those verses. But by the end of my stay at TSC I could quote them as well as the *Jesus Christ Superstar* lyrics I knew by heart.

The original set card

Sometimes mimeographed outlines were handed out before a class. Even so, we took notes like maniacs and covered these pages with Scripture references. We also did a lot of underlining and note taking right in our Bibles. Soon the margins in my Bible were filled up as I added comments like "Wow!" or "go to Matthew 5!" Someone filled me in on the secret of good Bible notation: a BIC FINE POINT pen (I especially coveted the big fat blue one with a four-color selection.) It's astounding how quickly I learned to maneuver through all the Scriptures. I rummaged through the pages of my Bible so much it began to fall apart—I was a frequent flipper.

It wasn't long before I had a pouch for my Bible, pen and toothbrush—just like the older brothers in the Family. Speaking of older brothers, all us babes were assigned an older brother buddy who kept watch over us. Their purpose wasn't to keep us captive or follow us around like we were in some communist reeducation camp. Our older brothers cared for us just like a real older brother. My buddy was Obediah—a homely, loose-limbed guy with stringy hair that kept falling into his face. He also possessed a thick lower lip that didn't seem to match his upper lip. Obediah didn't exactly drool, but periodically he had to suck up his spit as he spoke.

Appearances aside, this guy really knew his stuff and quoted Scripture like nobody's business. Obediah usually sat with me during meals and we often walked around the ranch during our free time as he shared his knowledge and vision. He constantly drilled me on my Bible verses and showed me how to write them down on index cards and for easy review. He also quizzed me about topics. *Where does it talk about grace verses works? Where does it talk about the anti-Christ? What are the signs that Jesus is returning soon? What's a good verse for this? What is a good verse for that?*

Obediah taught me practical stuff, too. *If you hang your underwear up at night to air out, you can wear that pair for a whole week. If you know the right technique, there's a fine art of taking a "bath" with just one pitcher of water. If you're too busy to wash your hair, just put baby powder on your head, rub it in and shake it out. But never wash your hair with a regular bar of soap…trust me, it's nasty.* I couldn't have asked for a better mentor. Obediah had high expectations for me—but man, I really loved the guy.

As our lessons progressed, we eventually got around to the heavy stuff: *End Time Bible Prophecy*. This took shape as we studied Old Testament books like Daniel and New Testament books like Revelation. By the end of these lessons I was totally convinced, along with everyone else in the group, that we were living in the Last Days of Earth's history. Based on the verses we studied, it seemed quite clear that Jesus was coming back soon—probably during our lifetime. This was both scary and exciting at the same time: scary because of the dire events that would happen before the end, but exciting because we would soon see the Lord coming in the clouds with great glory.

While the Children of God did not make any specific time predictions, we all believed there was *NOT MUCH TIME LEFT!* The Family had detailed, illustrated charts for the dreams and visions found in the prophetic books of the Bible. Before the return of Christ, specific events would take place. We were taught that after the fall of America, ten nations would unite to form a final one-world government on the earth, setting the stage for the anti-Christ. This marks the beginning of a

Me on the front row.

seven-year period before the world's end. At first the anti-Christ brings peace and is hailed as a great leader; however, in the middle of the seven years, the anti-Christ claims to be God and demand the worship of the world. Those submitting to the anti-Christ will be given the "mark of the beast" (the number 666), enabling them to buy and sell goods.

Those refusing to worship the anti-Christ will be hunted down and executed during the last three and a half years of Earth's history—the "Great Tribulation." After this period of extreme persecution and suffering, Jesus will return in the clouds and gather his beloved church in the air, giving them new bodies and taking them to heaven. Meanwhile, the anti-Christ will marshal his forces for the great "Battle of Armageddon." Of course, the returning heavenly forces will slaughter the satanic army and usher in a thousand-year reign of Christ on the Earth—the "Millennium." Following this comes the "White Throne Judgment" when the dead are raised to receive either rewards in heaven or punishment in hell.

Okay, I know all you prophecy nuts will say I've left out a whole bunch of details. But those are the broad strokes. If I charted it all out—who knows—you might start stocking up on canned goods. It may seem kooky, but back in 1970 a guy named Hal Lindsey published his book: The Late Great Planet Earth. Lots of Christians embraced the idea that they were living in the End Times. But I don't think any other group took it as far as the Children of God. This was serious stuff. In fact, it seemed like Bible prophecy was coming to pass before our very eyes. It was 1971 and I asked, "Will we even last until the end of this year before we see the anti-Christ rise?" All of these factors made us believe we were cutting-edge Christians, just like disciples of Jesus should be. Why waste your time on your education or career? You better repent and get saved while you can. And then you better get out and spread the word. The end is near!

It was a big deal with the Family that Christians had to go through the "Great Tribulation." This opposed the popular teaching of the day that all Christians will be raptured—taken away—to heaven before the shit hits the fan. The Family had particular scorn for a certain Scofield Bible that promoted what we considered the disgusting false doctrine called pre-tribulation rapture. We all had Matthew 24 marked up in case we encountered someone who wanted to argue this point. Seems like a little thing to squabble over, but it was a vital part of our mindset—we had to be trained and prepared for the reign of the Anti-Christ. So, here's the formula: (1) a steady diet of intense Bible classes, (2) euphoric group prayer sessions, (3) and then throw in "It's the end of the world! What have you got? Rocket fuel for our Jesus jet packs."

We all developed strong relationships during the basic Babe's Ranch training program. We were united with each other like soldiers going through boot camp. Whenever we met someone new, we immediately shared our testimonies. We swapped our new Biblical insights with the excitement of trading precious jewels. You were almost always with someone, but it was not forced on us—we liked it that way. I guess it was a natural transition for those of us coming out of the drug culture. Dopers form a special group, speaking their own insider's lingo, united by a bond of common experience. But in the Family we exclaimed, "I'm high on Jesus." We passed around Bible verses instead of joints. Our whole lives became a mind-bending trip.

EARLY ON I STARTED RECORDING my personal impressions.

I wanted to keep track of my new life, my lessons, and even dreams. It started out as notes written on random pieces of paper. Then someone gave me one of those little diary booklets. I called it my journal and it traveled with me everywhere. Writing in it was like a therapy session. I thought things out on paper and recorded good times and bad, victories and trials. When I eventually travelled around the country, I recorded my movements with dates and locations. I won't bore you with all my journal entries because they are mostly about Bible verses and personal revelations. But I will include some that enhance my story. Here is one from the early days:

Journal Entry, TSC (March 1971) Last night during inspiration a new convert named Jeremy got up with an electric guitar and played a beautiful song he wrote. He played the slide guitar and

it was far out. When we lined up for snack he was behind me and I introduced myself. He was a skinny little Brit and seemed as overwhelmed as I was when I first joined. So I gave him some encouragement as best I could. Later a brother told me he was Jeremy Spencer and had dropped out of a rock group called Fleetwood Mac to join the Family. I never heard of that band.

It was a struggle adjusting to this drug-free environment. After years of dope, sometimes the downward pull got intense. But we were taught to fight against negative feelings. Anything that got you down was considered an attack of the enemy. In such a case you could either say, "I'm having a battle" or "I'm going through a trial." The solution was prayer, quoting verses, or getting counsel from an older brother. I remember a song we sang about it:

When you joined the Lord's Army
Musta been lots of things you didn't realize
You're faced with your first battle
And you acted so darned surprised

It was common for new members to discuss their struggles with the leadership. Our Babe's Ranch leader, Joab, regularly gave inspirational pep talks encouraging us to persevere in our radically changed lives. I had happily joined the other Lost Boys in Never-Never Land, but when reality set in, doubts besieged me. *Had I made a mistake? What possessed me to drop out of school? I wanted to give my life to God, but did it have to be out in the middle of nowhere? But what would happen if I went back to my old systemite way of life?* (People outside of our group were called "Systemites" because they were part of the "Devil's System.")

After moping around for half a day, I made my way to Joab's trailer to talk it out.

He listened patiently and then said, "Right now you may think if you went back to your old way of life you would be happy. But if you do backslide and leave the Family, you will have a big hole in your soul.

You can try to fill it with things, but they won't satisfy you. That hole can only be filled by obedience to God. You have found the greatest treasure—serving Jesus. Will you exchange that for worldly pleasure? This is your real family. You have to fight the devil and his lies."

Joab wrapped his arms around me and prayed fervently. I could feel the love of true brotherhood flowing between us. A weight lifted off me and I could breathe again. I was delivered (at least for the time being). And this was an important theme in the Family: the fight against the desires of the flesh and the allure of the world.

An event took place shortly after this talk that made Joab's words ring true. A young man walked into the dining room and created quite a ruckus. He was bawling his head off and could barely get a word out. Some people knew him and went to his side and comforted him. When at last he calmed down, he told everyone how he left the Children of God about a year back. He returned to his girlfriend and got married. But things were hard for him because he felt guilty about being a backslider. He tried turning back to Jesus, but his wife would have nothing to do with religion and split. After that, he lost his job and had to live in his car. Finally, a major car accident almost cost his life. That gave him a clear message: *I need to repent and go back to my real family.* The prodigal son had returned and there was great rejoicing.

FREQUENTLY, JOAB WOULD READ US letters from a "friend."

At first I didn't know who this friend could be. Later, someone clued me in that these letters came from the founder of the Children of God—someone named Moses, or Mo for short. I knew TSC was not the only Children of God colony, so I assumed this Moses fellow lived at one of the other sites. I looked forward to meeting him someday.

The first Mo Letter I remember hearing was called "Diamonds of Dust." Mo observed how the rays of sunlight coming in his window made the floating dust particles sparkle like diamonds. Mo wrote:

"The diamonds of dust don't work hard to sparkle and shine. They

just let the light shine through them. They just float quietly on God's air and only get stirred up when He blows up a storm. Let your dust become diamonds that show the beauty of God."

We also enjoyed it when Joab read Bible chapters to us, followed by his commentary. One afternoon, while reading from Ezekiel, something happened that would have major consequences. I remember that meeting clearly. Joab came to a certain passage and suddenly lifted up his arms, praising God and speaking in tongues. We all started praising the Lord because we thought anything Joab gets excited about had to be important.

Journal Entry, TSC (April 1971) Joab read us the part of Ezekiel where it says there will be a future David who will be a king and shepherd. Joab got this look on his face like an angel just whispered in his ear. Then he told us something really heavy. Mo's real name is David and he is our king and shepherd! Wow! What a mindblower.

And sure enough, it wasn't long before Mo started using the name "Moses David." The slippery slope we were on became even more slippery. As the months went by at TSC, I heard lots of stories about David Berg. Older brothers passed down his background like an oral history from the elders of the tribe to the younger generation—the legend of Mo. It was an impressive collection of tales, all of which I totally bought into.

We were told that Mo's mother—Virginia Brandt Berg—was a well-known evangelist in California. We even listened to tapes of her old radio program called "Meditation Moments." When you heard her sweet voice, you loved her right away. Her sermonettes were encouraging messages to trust in the Lord. She also wrote a book entitled *The Hem of His Garment* describing how she was miraculously raised from her sick bed after a prayer of faith. Then she dedicated her life to the Lord and became an evangelist. (If you got sick in the Family, this book was required reading.) Even though she was long dead, we all called her "Grandmother Berg."

David Berg traveled with his mother as a companion. Later, hoping to succeed in the family business, he went off and pastored a small church. According to Mo's version, he was kicked out of his position because he told the church members they should use their church building as a kind of shelter and soup kitchen for the poor. When the church gig fell through, Mo started working for a televangelist named Fred Jordan who had a television ministry in California called "Church in the Home." Mo traveled around with his family and promoted the program. Eventually Jordan bought a ranch in Texas and converted it into a training center for Christians—the "Texas Soul Clinic."

David Berg with his first wife and four children.

When his employment with Jordan ended, Mo hauled his family around the country in a travel trailer. He observed the vibrant youth culture in California and started visiting hippie hangouts looking like a wild-eyed prophet (with a beard, black beret, T-shirt, jeans, sunglasses and sandals.) Mo preached about Jesus and was surprised when several young people not only became converted to Christianity, but also joined him in his travels. Soon a small caravan of disciples in vans and cars followed Mo, going from park to park, city to city. That was the start of the Family.

David Berg (Mo)

Mo often took his little band to a church on Sundays. At times he would stand up in the middle of the service to correct something in the sermon. This was not well received (no shit) and the group was often forcibly ejected. That was considered a good day because then Mo and his small band of disciples could rejoice about suffering persecution.

A newspaper reporter once wrote a story about the Family while they camped out in a local park. In the somewhat favorable piece the reporter called the group "The Children of God." The name stuck. When the wagon train of cars, vans and trailers became too large, Mo asked his old boss, Fred Jordan, for the use of his now abandoned Texas Soul Clinic property. In the Family's lingo, Jordan became a "King" (a term used for rich guys who helped out the group with donations or places to live.) And that explains the

letterhead at the top of the papers I used to write my parents while at TSC.

With TSC as a base camp, Mo sent teams out to start colonies in other cities. I don't know the exact date, but somewhere in there Mo got one of his revelations from God instructing him to travel around the world in secret. It all had something to do with him being free from all the distractions of day-to-day leadership so he could dedicate himself totally to his inspirational and instructional writings for the Family. I think Mo was also paranoid about his safety (whether real or imagined.) Not many details were given, but it sounded very adventurous and in line with our radical revolution for Jesus.

Mo took along his young secretary, Maria, as a companion on his travels. She became Mo's second wife after he had—you guessed it— another revelation from God. Mo claimed that the Lord told him he needed a new, more revolutionary wife.

His second wife was supposed to be a symbol of Mo's calling as God's end time prophet. This whole wife swap was explained in a Mo Letter called Old Love, New Love.

Here is a snippet:

> *She shall be clothed in a new garment and a new look and all things shall become new and old things shall pass away and I will have a new bride who will love me and obey me and do my will.*

This is Maria before her departure from TSC.

After Joab's big revelation from the book of Ezekiel about the David prophecy, he promptly sent a letter to Mo and announced his inspiration: *Our Moses is actually the David prophesied in the Bible.* At first Mo rejected the notion, but later came to embrace it. Here's an excerpt from a Mo Letter entitled "David" written on June 20, 1971:

The cover of the
David Mo Letter

A few months ago, one of you wrote me and got all excited about Ezekiel 34 and said the Lord had showed him this was about me! I tried to laugh it off, but I was frightened about it... that maybe it was true! I tried to brush it off and accredit it to the overzealous loyalty of one of my most overbearing generals. But... I prayed about it... and last night the Lord told me what He thought about it... straight from His own Mouth! The Lord rebuked me, "Why dost thou deny thy name David? You have doubted that I am able to do this... but I have made thee My Moses and My David!"

So what about Mo's first wife and the mother of his four children? Surprisingly, she stuck around. Everyone affectionately called her "Mother Eve" and the Family held her in great esteem. (As a consolation prize Eve likewise took on a younger companion named Stephen.)

Whenever one of the Mo letters came in, it was read aloud to the whole assembled body. Then the letter was typed up and published for all the other colonies. At first they were mimeographed on pretty cheap paper. Later some guy in the print shop shrunk them down to the size of an index card. We punched a hole in the top left corner of our collections and fasten them on a metal ring—something new to dangle from our pouches. Much later the Mo Letters were distributed in pamphlet form

(5.5 X 8.5 inches) and finally they were published in a book that looked suspiciously like a Bible.

So what did the Mo Letters contain? At first they were inspirational and encouraging messages about our lives as revolutionary Christians. Occasionally, Mo communicated rebukes for things he didn't like. But that was okay because we all thought we were hearing from a loving father who cared about us.

Our artists started depicting Mo as a lion. Go figure!

I was told that after Mo's departure, some zealous leaders decided it would be cool if everyone spoke in King James English. A month or so went by as people attempted this.

"How art thou, my brother?"

"I doeth well."

"May your day be blessed."

"Thine as well, beloved."

And on it went until Mo got wind of it and called it off.

Somebody else had another bright idea to organize the Family into tribes like the Israelites in the Old Testament. That was actually still going on while I was there at TSC. I only remember a few of them. The tribe of Levi was for the leaders. The tribe of Simeon was for the cooks and kitchen helpers. The tribe of Benjamin was for the people who cared for the children. The tribe of Gad was for the print shop workers. After I left TSC, I didn't hear much about the tribal system. It died a natural death and was buried next to the King James English disaster.

When I joined, there were about 500 Children of God members scattered around the USA in five or six colonies. Obediah told me, "Someday you can proudly say you were one of the first 500." A few Family members at TSC were pointed out as "original disciples" who joined Mo in California. I really envied them for that honor.

So, it seemed we had a King... our own King David. And very soon it dawned on us we also had a Queen... and her name was Maria. As the Family grew bigger and bigger, Maria's role expanded. This was the beginning of a very slippery slope. Just wait... you will see.

May 1971 to June 1972

"Aha!" said the puppet. "Look how I can walk.
Now I have a voice. Just listen to me talk.
I want to be more than just a wooden toy.
I hope that one day I will be a real boy!"

HEAVY BROTHER

WHEN MAY ROLLED AROUND, I moved out of the Babes' Ranch. With the required basic training under my belt, it was time to put me to work. No longer a babe, but not yet an older brother, it was sort of an in-between state. I was kept busy with a variety of chores. I especially enjoyed helping in the kitchen with food prep or washing dishes because you got to swap tales with the other workers.

Occasionally I was drafted for guard duty. Since we were taught to expect persecution, it was natural to put some kind of alarm system in place in case a truckload of anti-Christ enemies rolled up to our front gate in the middle of the night. There was this old broken down car sitting on top of a hill overlooking the entrance to our camp. This was called "Mobile One." It was outfitted with a walkie-talkie to communicate with "Mobile Two"—another guard post watching the backside of the camp.

If you were on guard duty you stayed up all night, ready to warn everyone if worse came to worst. To keep us going, we would receive a plate of sandwiches, doughnuts and coffee. While waiting for the devil to launch an attack on the camp, you got to read your Bible with a flashlight, have a midnight snack, and chat with the other guard post on the walkie-talkie. For sure, this was some thrilling boy stuff. The only down side was finding a place to sleep the next day. With all the hustle and bustle—not to mention the heat—you could only get a catnap.

Apart from those extra chores, my main job was working in the print shop. I liked being in there with all the machines going. On top of that they always had music or scripture tapes blasting away. I had never been so busy in my life, working harder than I ever had before, sometimes all night when things got tight. So how come I loved it so much?

That's me in the front, working with the printer.

66

One week I heard about a bus team being put together for a weekend witnessing trip in Dallas. I was very excited and hoped to be chosen for the expedition. When I saw my name on the list, I almost exploded with joy. The thought of going out and sharing the good news with lost souls was delightful. Waiting for Saturday to arrive was like waiting for Christmas.

When that day came, we all packed into the bus, loaded for bear. Got Bibles? Check! Got Tracts? Check!

While on the road we sang our hearts out, listened to witnessing tips from older brothers, and practiced our memory verses. When we got to a Dallas park, we were sent out in teams of two. It didn't take me long to find out not everyone wanted to get saved. Many people we targeted shut us down as soon as they heard us mention Jesus. Some laughed at us, especially if they had some buddies around them. But lots of folks listened to our verses and engaged in some pretty intense discussions. That night we all gathered at the bus, shared our testimonies, and rejoiced over every soul won to Christ.

Someone took this picture of me witnessing in the park.

It seemed like my sojourn at the Texas Soul Clinic lasted a long time, but I was only there in February, March, April and May. It was like my memory of elementary school recesses—they always felt longer than they actually were. I became attached to lots of guys at TSC, but their names wouldn't mean anything to you—Jeremiah, Jacob, Sampson, Simon, Mordecai... see what I mean? There were also plenty of girls at TSC—we called them sisters, naturally. Some were married, but most were single. All of them had long hair and wore long dresses. Being eighteen, I would eye every girl I met as a future marital prospect. That was my dream—to serve the Lord together with a partner. But it never went any further than random thoughts flitting through my head. Considering my life before the Family, it's hard to believe I was so chaste.

It didn't take long for me to figure out who was the top leader at TSC. It was Jethro, who would appear in the evenings to give fatherly exhortations to the whole assembly. He was married to Deborah, David Berg's oldest daughter. She created a little school modeled on the Montessori Method. Deborah and Jethro would become major players in my not-too-distant future—especially the Montessori bit.

Jethro, Deborah and the Montessori Kids.

At the end of May, Jethro told me about a colony up near the small Texas town of Merkel. It was an advanced training course with even more Bible studies. He wanted to know if I was interested in moving there. Since Merkel was in redneck country, I would have to get a short haircut. Nevertheless, it sounded great to me. My hair wasn't that long anyway.

The next morning I got a buzz cut and packed myself in a van with three other guys. As we drove away I could hear someone yell our standard parting phrase, "Be seeing you—here, there or in the air." As we passed through the front gate, I looked back fondly at the ranch where I had come to know and love many brothers and sisters. For the next 13 months I bounced around the United States going from one colony to another.

IT WAS A LONG, HOT and dusty ride to the Merkel colony.

We finally arrived at this little house way out in the boonies. Come to think of it, I'm not sure I ever saw the town of Merkel. We drove up and were greeted by several brothers and one sister. Banai and his wife (pictured below) were in charge of the place. All the other colony members were male.

Like Joab at TSC, Banai was a combination leader and Bible teacher. He was a tall, slender, dark-haired guy with a rather intense face. But Banai and his wife were nice folks and tried hard to make do with what little they had to work with. I felt loved and blessed to be under their care. Even though it was very hot—and we had no air conditioning—I have some fond memories of the place. Too bad my time there was cut short (for reasons that will soon become clear.)

We would rise early for morning devotions. These usually consisted of selected readings from Psalms and Proverbs. We had this system where we read the chapter from the book of Proverbs corresponding with the day's date. On May 3rd, we read Proverbs chapter 3. This worked out nicely since the book of Proverbs has 31 chapters. It didn't work with the Psalms, so we just read as many as we had time for.

Then we all did a few chores. There were few trees or bushes around the house, so we were constantly dusting. The front living room had a thin, threadbare carpet and we would sprinkle water on it and use a broom to sweep it. That raised clouds of dust, but worked pretty well. I remember thinking, *"Who needs a vacuum cleaner?"* And Banai's wife would occasionally enlist us to help in her valiant attempt at growing a vegetable garden. Sadly, it didn't yield much. (Wait! I think we did have peas from the garden for one meal.)

After breakfast, we would gather for a Bible class in the living room. The house was so small that the kitchen crew—whoever was washing the dishes or working on dinner—could still hear the lesson. I can still picture them stepping in with their aprons on so they could add something to the discussion. It was a charming arrangement. Banai was a maniac for end time Bible prophecy and had a knack for bringing it to life. His teaching style was to cover a few verses and then open it up for questions or comments. Since we were all familiar with the material, this was a stimulating time to whip out our well-marked and cross-referenced Bibles and bat around ideas and theories. If you came up with a good verse or interesting insight you had the pleasure of hearing Banai say, "That's heavy, brother."

Once at TSC, after a new convert gave his testimony, someone called out to him, "Who witnessed to you?"

So this babe goes, "It was Samuel."

There was a murmur of approval from the crowd and someone next to me said, "Do you know Samuel? He's a heavy brother."

I thought, *"Someday I want to be a heavy brother."* Isn't that what we all want, to have weight, to be valued?

After dinner we would have the customary inspiration—that time of singing, praising God and praying. Just like at TSC, this was followed by free time for personal study, letter writing and so on. But occasionally Banai would read us Mo Letters or give inspirational talks. One evening he surprised us with a cautionary lecture on the temptation of masturbation.

"It's a carnal urge you must resist. I know each and every one of you boys in this room struggle with this sin. If you say you haven't indulged, then I know you're lying."

All the brothers were silent—no one wanted to risk being called a liar. But the truth was that since joining the Family, the thought of stroking it never crossed my mind. To be sure, I was no stranger to the practice. Like most teenage boys I mastered the practice of jacking off as soon as my equipment became functional. Yet in all the busy days of exciting revolutionary activities, my mind was filled with other things.

But at bedtime—having been reminded of my former hobby—the serpent reared its ugly head. All verses, lectures and self-righteous postures deserted me. My mind was hit by relentless waves of desire. I yielded and plucked that forbidden fruit from the tree and took a ravenous bite. It was a sweet but short-lived pleasure after which I fell into depths of condemnation. I knew I was naked and ashamed in the garden—no longer pure.

Journal Entry, Merkel (June 1971) I asked God to forgive me and deliver me from this thorn in my flesh. I know God will help me get the victory. But I'm going through a trial about it. Lord, help me walk in the Spirit and not mind the things of the flesh.

As a good shepherd, Banai felt it was his duty to prepare us for the coming Great Tribulation during which Christians would be hunted down, tortured and killed for their faith. Banai would terrorize us with tales of what we could expect: beatings, fingernails ripped off, getting sawed in half or burned alive (I could go on… it was kind of like Christian torture porn). He also read us excerpts from a book entitled *Tortured for*

Christ by Richard Wurmbrand who was a Christian minister captured by the communists and persecuted for his faith back in the Cold War/Iron Curtain days. His book described the torture and pain he endured. It made for a rather grim bedtime story and gave me nightmares.

It reminded me of the time when one of my aunts took me and my cousins to a triple feature horror movie at the drive in. My cousins were teenage boys at the time, but I was only seven. As these low-budget blood-fest movies were projected into my childish brain, I went into a kind of shock. One of the movies (*The Horror of the Black Museum*) had a scene where a maniac sneaked into a lady's home and set up a guillotine behind her bed. When she put her head on the pillow, she looked up and saw the blade—but (whack) it was too late. Put to bed in my cousins' room, I was so terrified I stayed awake all night. Even back at home I was unable to sleep in my own room until I went through an elaborate ritual of looking under my bed (any sharp cutting instruments?) and carefully examining my closet (any maniacs in there?) Once in bed I tucked the blankets around my neck (somehow a magical protection from decapitation.)

But now I had God on my side for protection. I thought we prayed a lot at TSC, but Banai took us up to the next level. We were exhorted to pray before absolutely everything we did. Time to eat? *Lord, bless the food.* Running an errand in the car? *Lord, keep us safe on the road and help the car not to break down.* We even prayed before putting letters into the mailbox. *Lord, help this to reach its destination.* (Apparently the devil loved playing little tricks like stalling our cars and diverting our mail.)

I don't know how people heard about us since we weren't exactly in the center of a metropolis, but we did get the occasional visitors. They would just trickle in and we would be all Texas friendly, invite them in for a chat, sing a few songs for them and give them a glass of ice tea. Mostly these folks heard we were some kind of church group and felt it was their duty to set us straight about their pet doctrinal points. (We considered them to be religious nuts since only the Children of God had the real truth.)

After about six weeks I came down with an illness that gave me a horrible sore throat and painful swollen glands in my neck. It was very hard for me to eat solid foods and I wound up in bed. The whole colony strenuously prayed for my healing and I confessed all the sins I could think of that might be blocking God's power, but my condition worsened. One day Banai came into the room, wept over me and then—like the prophet Elisha in the Old Testament—spread himself prostrate on top of me, begging for the Lord to raise me up. However, no miracle was forthcoming.

Journal Entry, Merkel (July 1971) I am tired of being sick. Last night I prayed that God would do whatever it took to make me what He wants me to be. It made me scared to pray such a prayer and now I don't know what will happen. But I am in the Lord's hands.

Days passed and I was losing weight. A skinny teenager to begin with, I went from 125 pounds to about 100. My tongue was now white with a nasty red, raw crack down the middle. At that point Banai got worried and called for reinforcements. And who should come to my rescue? Mother Eve herself. She was not the leader of any colony, but travelled around inspiring the troops and trouble-shooting. When Mother Eve heard about my sad condition, she whisked me away to her current location in Houston. Banai got chastised for letting it get so bad. I felt sorry for him because it was my fault for not having enough faith to be healed. Poor Banai was just following the playbook.

ONCE IN HOUSTON MY CONDITION cleared up mysteriously.

Mother Eve ordered the brethren to feed me double portions and in time I gained most of my weight back. I didn't discover until years later—after leaving the Family—that my illness was the first onset of a lifelong sensitivity to dust. (So much for sweeping carpets.)

After my recovery, I went to the Dallas colony. The Family's printing operation had been moved from TSC to Dallas and they needed workers. Someone in Dallas heard that I worked in the print shop at TSC and sent me the invitation. The new print facility was located on the second floor of a warehouse. We walked up some narrow stairs to get to a workspace about as big as a basketball court. When I looked at all the massive machines, I wondered how they squeezed them through such a little passageway. I was told the machines were taken apart piece by piece and then reassembled upstairs.

They put me to work in the shipping department—just a corner, really—where I packed up bundles of literature to send out to the various colonies around the country. From Dallas we distributed Mo Letters, tracts, postcards and cassette tapes of the Family's music.

We printed lots of these "Warning Tracts."

The print shop workers were housed in various "off campus" facilities. One such place was an abandoned home we all called the "free house." One look was enough to see why—the structure leaned to one side and part of the roof was missing. The uneven floors made it seem like a carnival fun house. But the Family took it as a challenge and began the repairs. I arrived when the job was half done. Sleeping there felt precarious.

All the single brothers in Dallas used sleeping bags. We didn't have our own bedroom or even an assigned bed for that matter. I slept on a bed when one was available; but other times I made do with the floor. I just rolled up my coat to use as a pillow. Those were the days when I could sleep almost anywhere.

We had not been able to go out witnessing regularly at TSC or Merkel, but things were different in Dallas. The weather was nice and there were plenty of parks where we could go to preach the Gospel. Happiness was my main conversation starter.

"Are you happy with the way your life is going? Would you like to be happier than you ever thought possible?"

This was not just a tactic on my part—I said it with all sincerity. At that time I was genuinely happy. My head was loaded with hundreds of Bible verses; and telling other people about Jesus seemed totally natural. What could be better? Being out in the field was like combat training. Sure, I got rejected a lot; but that just made me sharper in my next skirmish.

Once I came across this guy sitting next to a tree with his nose in a book. He must have been into Philosophy 101 because after hearing my pitch he said, "You claim to have the truth? I don't believe in absolute truth."

"You don't believe in truth?"

"I don't believe in absolutes. There are no absolutes."

"Are you absolutely sure about that?"

He got my point and laughed. We talked for quite a while, but in the end he still didn't accept Jesus.

After two months of packing boxes and thick envelopes in Dallas, a leader told everyone about a new colony in Colorado that needed workers. One night I was talking to a sister named Asenath and told her

I was thinking about going there.

She exclaimed, "This is a confirmation of the Lord's leading because I have a burden to go to Colorado!" ("Burdens" were desires laid on your heart by God as guidance.)

After getting permission from leadership, it only took a day for me to train someone to take my place at the print shop. Asenath and I had to make our way to Colorado on our own—no one was going to drive us or fork out money for bus tickets. In the Family's jargon, this was called a "faith trip." You just went out—usually with only pocket change to use for the phone in case of an emergency—and took only what you could carry.

Journal Entry, Dallas (September 1971) Jabin helped us get ready for the trip. He spread out a big road map of the USA and charted out a route. He said it was a good plan to go through cities with colleges because it was usually pretty easy to find places to crash.

Early the next morning Jabin drove us to Fort Worth where he knew a good spot to start hitchhiking. And he was right—we got our first ride in a few minutes. Getting rides was pretty easy. You just stood there on the side of the road, stuck out your thumb and tried not to look like an ax murderer. Several vans picked us up (the official cool vehicle for long-haired freaks). We did have one bad experience with a couple of cowboys in a huge Pontiac. As we rode along in the back seat, the jerks up front kept making lewd comments about Asenath and telling her they could really give her the ride of her life. We did not tell these guys about Jesus. As soon as they stopped for gas, we jumped out.

We passed through Wichita Falls and Amarillo, both in Texas. Then we clipped the northeast corner of New Mexico and passed through Pueblo. When we reached Colorado we went through Colorado Springs and Denver before arriving at our destination outside Boulder. These cities had colleges of various sizes and, sure enough, lots of college kids shared their dorms with us. One night I slept in the back of a car while Asenath stayed in a girls' apartment. I didn't mind—it was better than the floor. The meals just kind of happened. Folks would treat us or give us a few bucks. Of course, whoever picked us up got an ear full. We wanted them to know they would get a blessing for helping us.

We soon discovered we weren't the only game in town—we met lots of Jesus People. You could find them sharing housing, especially in college towns. We even crashed at a Jesus People dwelling on our trek. When I went inside there were banners with verses all over the place. Jesus people dressed like they were a blend—part hippie and part straight. (Back then "straight" simply meant "not hip" and had nothing to do with sexuality.) They wore necklaces with big crosses, passed out lots of tracts, and mostly invited kids back to their place to talk. Their mission was to save people and get them to clean up their lives. One of their tracts looked like a little comic book illustrating the story of a longhaired guy—surely strung out on drugs—being witnessed to. He received Jesus and the last picture showed him singing in church with short hair and dressed all clean cut. We had a lot in common with the Jesus People, but our end game was definitely not attending church. The Family taught that the believers were the church, not a building. We said, "We don't GO to church; we ARE the church." This anti-establishment message appealed to young folks who had negative experiences in church.

By the time we reached the Colorado colony the weather was getting crisp. The colony layout reminded me a bit of TSC, but the buildings were in better shape. The main house was a large two-story structure. The mountains in view around the colony were magnificent. I remember the water there was the best I ever had—it tasted almost sweet coming right out of the faucets.

Because I had completed the Family's basic training, I was put to work instead of attending classes. Meanwhile, I was really getting a handle on the Bible. In those days you could read me a verse and I could tell you what book of the Bible it came from down to the chapter and verse. I was not unique. We all poured over Scriptures for hours.

There was room on the side of the house used as a Greeting Room. Every day two Family members were posted there to welcome visitors. Since the greeters provided a public relations front, they dressed nicer than the average colony member. Some visitors just came to check out the Jesus freaks, but others were genuine truth seekers. We also got quite a few parents worried about what their kids had gotten themselves into.

Greeters presented the Family in the best possible light, answering questions, calming the fears of anxious relatives, and witnessing to hungry souls. Not long after I arrived in Colorado I was asked to work as a greeter.

Since I had learned how to flim-flam adults at an early age, I was a natural in the greeting room. It's not that I dished out a pack of lies; I just kept back certain things about the Family. Of course, I would never say something like, "Oh, by the way, our founder is a great prophet named Moses who travels around in secret. Never met him but we love and obey him." No, that information was for members only. But I had plenty of other material that was safe for general consumption. All in all it was an easy gig. There were waves of visitors on the weekends, but mostly I did a lot of sitting around and waiting. When a guest arrived I would shift into gear and rattle off my lines.

"We are a group of young Christians who follow Jesus as the disciples did in the Bible, forsaking all our former evil ways in order to serve the Lord fulltime. Our goal is to go all over the world and preach about Jesus. We live in communities like the early church did in the book of Acts. We are not wild-eyed terrorists. We are not radical communists. We are not free-love hippies. We do love you, though, and hope you will accept Christ into your heart. Would you like some tea or coffee? We also have fresh baked cookies."

While working as a greeter I developed my own style, avoiding some of the extreme witnessing strategies I had observed. Once David Z. was ridiculed by a guy who said, "You are just using Jesus as a crutch."

David Z. fired back, "Jesus isn't my crutch. He's my WHEELCHAIR!"

Another time Cephas went up to a guy sitting on a park bench strumming his guitar. As soon as Cephas started talking about God, the guy cut him off.

"Don't give me that stuff about a God in heaven handing down rules. We're all the result of evolution, survival of the fittest, man."

Cephas goes, "You don't believe in rules?"

"Nah! Just do your own thing."

Cephas put his hand on this guy's guitar and said, "This is a nice instrument. I think I'll take it from you. After all, no rules, right?"

The dude yanked away his guitar and stalked off.

As for me, I preferred a lighter touch. My main approach was to listen and ask a bunch of questions. You'd be surprised what people will reveal when they have an eager audience. This would often give me a lead on how to introduce the Gospel.

My partner in the greeting room was a pretty sister named Jael. We got along well and enjoyed chatting during the lulls. As you can imagine, it didn't take long for me to begin wondering if this could be the girl for me. As the weeks went by we became more comfortable with each other's company and I developed a little crush on her. That was nothing new for me—I had fantasies about all the single sisters. But I left it at that because, as you recall, no dating (or smooching) was allowed in the Family. The most a guy could do was to show off his awesome spirituality, like a peacock spreading his tail feathers, and see what would happen.

Marriage in the Family worked like this: if two members became romantically inclined they would first approach leadership for prayer and counsel to get the Lord's leading. Leaders weren't shy about splitting people up if it didn't seem like a good match. Only couples considered *strong in the Lord* were candidates for marriage. If you passed the test, leadership would allow you to spend time with each other taking walks, reading the Bible together or sitting together for meals—innocent stuff like that. After an indeterminate waiting period, if all signs remained positive, the couple came before the whole colony for a betrothal ceremony. And that was it—you were hitched (at least in the eyes of the Family). However, after the consummation, married couples were encouraged to get a legal marriage.

I can't actually remember who was the main shepherd at the Colorado colony because there were lots of big cheeses running around. One of them I remembered from TSC, a rather eccentric fellow named Jacob Cartoon. He not only drew cartoons for various Family publications, but he also acted kind of like a cartoon character. Anyway, one day he was talking to the colony members about the commitment and perseverance required for marriage. Then he laughed and said, "If you marry in haste you may repent at leisure!"

That was food for thought. Should I explore the subject with Jael? A week later I was in the greeting room and Jael didn't show up. Someone came in and said, "Jael went missing last night. We found out today she ran off and is now back at home with her parents." I scratched that girl off my list.

I TOOK HOME ECONOMICS IN high school to get out of PE.

It turned out I really enjoyed the cooking classes. Even as a teenager I loved watching Julia Child on TV. She was "The French Chef" and I got a kick out of her quirky personality. It was fun to see how she turned a bunch of ingredients into a gourmet meal. I also used to watch the Jack LaLanne show. You know who that guy was? Probably not. But he was the original health and fitness guru who would go through exercise routines and demonstrate how to make healthy meals. He dressed in a tight, sleeveless one-piece exercise suit revealing his rippling muscles like a fitness superhero. So, between Home Economics, Julia Child and Jack LaLanne, I picked up a few things about cooking.

With that background, you can see why I was delighted when one of the leaders asked if I was interested in going to Detroit to take over as a cook in their kitchen. He said the position would prepare me for a leadership role because between cooking duties I would have plenty of time for personal study and prayer. Working as a cook in Detroit sounded like fun to me. After two months in Colorado I was on the road again.

I arrived in Detroit in November and found myself in a colony packed with a couple dozen brothers and sisters. Most of them were black. People may intellectually concur that skin color makes no difference; however, because of social structures, they have little opportunity to practice their beliefs and tear down racial walls. But communal living is a sure way to dissolve racial differences. Brothers and sisters…that's all we saw.

The kitchen overseer—who was leaving for another colony to be a Bible teacher—showed me the ins and outs of his kitchen in just one day. His secret weapon was his kitchen bible—a huge Betty Crocker cookbook with every recipe and cooking tip you could imagine. He also told me his secret about performing meal preparation quickly.

"Clean as you cook," he said. "Lots of people cook a meal and then clean up after. That turns it into two jobs and takes much longer. Instead, after you prep something and put it on to cook, clean up the dishes and the area you used. Your kitchen job will be shortened and you will have more free time for yourself."

I always wondered where all the Family's food came from. I knew each colony had a provisioning team that went out to local merchants in order to get contributions of food. But I never knew the nitty-gritty. Now, as a cook, it all became crystal clear. The Family mainly survived on food that was regularly tossed out by grocery stores and restaurants. We ate a heck of a lot of bread and pastries too old to keep on store shelves. We were also given any meat and vegetables that had passed the point of looking appetizing to picky American shoppers. But since I never knew exactly what would come in, I had to figure out how to get the most out of whatever was delivered to the kitchen.

So what do you do with a huge bag of old donuts? Sure, they could be served for breakfast and snacks, but combined with milk and other ingredients they make a delicious bread pudding. We also got in lots of those sandwiches they used to sell in vending machines. I took out the meat and cheese, but threw away the bread (okay, so maybe I ate a few of those sandwiches). Then I put the meat into soups, stews, meatloaf or casseroles. The cheese could be mixed with pasta or rice. And then there was my signature dish: *Frito Pie*. (Actually, that's a dish most Texans know about—just fill a pan with corn chips, dump cans of chili on top, sprinkle on cheese and bake it in the oven.)

Since butter was harder for us to lay our hands on, I used a "spread it on, scrape it off" method to give toast just a hint. If I got in crates of blueberries, then I put them in everything I could think of: blueberries in the pancakes, blueberries in the bread pudding and blueberries for cereal. You get the idea.

And it was true that I had lots of time for personal study. I really used it, going over all my old classes with a fine-tooth comb and memorizing lots of verses. I loved the Psalms and committed over a dozen of them to memory. In the New Testament I memorized several whole chapters from Matthew, John and Revelation. This was on top of the hundreds of single verses I already knew by heart. It's amazing what the brain of a teenager can accomplish.

I had good relations with the other Family members—when you are the cook it kind of comes with the territory. Occasionally I was let off my leash and allowed to go into town on witnessing trips. My favorite witnessing partner was a beautiful black sister named Jerusha, a hefty, full-figured girl with long curly hair. We used to get into buses or elevators, open our Bibles, and talk to each other loudly in the middle of the other riders.

"Look at what Jesus said (insert salvation verse here). Isn't that AWESOME?"

"Yes! Jesus died for us because (insert salvation verse here)."

If we felt led, we would sing a few Gospel songs. In those days we always kept "stats." When you came back from witnessing you reported how many people you spoke to, how many got saved, and any contacts you made for future follow-ups. The stats were compiled from every colony and we would receive regular updates from top leadership.

Journal Entry, Detroit (December 1971) Today I was out witnessing with Jerusha and this white lady approached us and said, "I just wanted to tell you how courageous you are being out in public like this." At first we thought she was talking about our witnessing, but then she said, "You rarely see a white guy with a black girl, at least not in Detroit." This lady thought we were out on a date and wanted to cheer us on. It turns out she was married to a black guy and had to endure quite a bit of prejudice.

I passed a very pleasant three months in Detroit. The house where we stayed was barely big enough for us. Most of the brothers slept on the bottom floor of the house—quite literally on the floor—but I got to sleep on a couch that was off to the side of the kitchen. The sisters all slept in rooms on the upper floor, but they had bunk beds. During my time there I prepared a major Christmas meal for our home and another colony nearby. So the provisioning team worked extra hard to procure my shopping list for turkey and the fixings for about 40 Family members. It was very satisfying to watch everyone eat the meal I slaved over. I was thinking, *"Maybe this is my calling... to be a Family cook."* But that wasn't meant to be. At the end of January 1972, I was told my cooking stint was over. A small colony in Kentucky needed a Bible teacher.

⁕⁕⁕⁕⁕⁕⁕⁕⁕⁕⁕⁕⁕⁕⁕⁕⁕⁕⁕⁕⁕⁕⁕⁕

THIS TIME I ACTUALLY GOT a ride all the way to Kentucky.

The colony shepherds, Nathanael and his wife Michal, greeted me warmly. I don't know why, but they called it the "Kentucky Farm." Thick woods surrounded the tumbledown cabin that looked like only fervent prayer held it up. Going through the backdoor I walked through the kitchen and into one big room on the bottom floor. It was sparsely furnished and had a pot-bellied stove in the middle. I went up some rickety stairs to get to a small attic space filled with bunk beds. That's where I would be sleeping with the other brothers. The sisters were fewer in number and had a little room downstairs. The entrance to their bedroom was just covered with a blanket—there was no door—but the men never thought of peeking inside.

We had electricity, but no running water. The brothers made daily trips down to a small spring waterfall that was a short hike from the house. Our toilet was an outhouse. Someone constructed a makeshift shower stall outside the house. You heated up water and poured it into this tin box with a shower attachment. However, because it was such a hassle to haul, heat and transfer the water, I mainly took sponge baths and washed my hair at the kitchen sink with a pitcher of water. When the weather got warmer, you could go down and bathe in the waterfall; but even in summer it was so cold it gave you a sex change in a matter of seconds.

Nathanael and Michal had an old broken-down bus next to the house for their bedroom and office. Nathanael was quite a character. I didn't know it then, but I heard much later he was a gay hair stylist before joining the Family. So-called gay mannerisms were not yet popularized in movies and on television, so I was clueless. I just thought Nathanael was very flamboyant. He tried hard to make a radical impression, perhaps copying other leaders he had been around. His wife and I soon became fast friends. Michal was easy to get along with and had a great

83

sense of humor. We shared many a laugh as we worked in the kitchen. Michal would tease me, "When are you going to get married, Salem? There are some cute sisters here at the Farm." (She found this more amusing than I did.)

The colony was a mini babes' ranch. So there I was, in charge of teaching a small number of new disciples their daily basic classes. Believe me, I was well prepared and went at it with gusto. Since we didn't have a supply of musicians, the group had to endure the small set of songs I could play on an ancient guitar someone gave me in Detroit. I mainly played the familiar Family songs, but I also wrote a couple of my own. (I still remember the tunes and chords.)

There was a beloved brother there, a sweet, spacey guy named Shaphat Muskrat. I'm sure he had a reason for the muskrat part, but I can't recall it. In those days Family members sometimes took second names to further identify themselves. At TSC there was a brother whose last name was *Parking Lot* because he worked in one when he met the Family. Anyway, Shaphat was the colony provisioner and made regular runs into town to do food pickups for our meals. I would see him dress up in a suit and tie and drive off in the colony vehicle. He would return in the evening with the car full of supplies. You never knew what he would bring back.

One day Shaphat pulled up and said excitedly, "I have a trunk full of Pee Cans." It was our practice to keep an empty can near our beds in case we needed to pee in the middle of the night—we dreaded that frigid walk to the outhouse. I don't know about the girls, but all the guys had a pee can. But even so, I couldn't understand why Shaphat was so thrilled about a trunk load of cans. When he opened up the trunk I saw big boxes of pecans (we don't pronounce it "pee can" in Texas).

Michal would usually go out provisioning with Shaphat, but one day Shaphat asked me to accompany him. We drove off in the morning and it was pretty much what I expected. We went to restaurants and grocery stores to pick up the food they would otherwise toss out. But on this outing I got a big surprise. Shaphat took me to a grocery store and said, "Salem, the manager here is a hard-hearted heathen and won't put anything aside for us. But we have a way around that."

He drove the car around to the back of the store and pulled up to a long line of metal dumpsters. I was surprised when Shaphat took off his jacket, climbed up on top of some crates and peered into the dumpster.

"Good stuff today," he said as he plucked out boxes of fruits, vegetables and even wrapped meats and cheeses. We worked our way down the line of dumpsters and made quite a haul. This was my first exposure to dumpster diving. It is shocking how much food is thrown away in America.

In February we got an influx of new disciples from "The Jesus People Army"—a group that merged with the Children of God. They rolled up in a recreational vehicle and parked next to the house. There were two married couples and some single brothers. The married couples bedded down in the camper while the brothers joined me up in the attic.

One day Nathanael told me, "I don't know if these babes are revolutionary enough. I think we should toughen them up."

"Really?" I replied. "I think they are all sweet and love Jesus with all their hearts."

"Is that right? Maybe you need to toughen up."

I thought all the babes were plenty revolutionary. One of my favorites was a brother named Orion. He had a heck of a testimony of being led to the Family during a massive meteor shower—kind of like the wise men being led to the baby Jesus. Orion was what we used to call an "on fire brother" and would witness to everyone he came in contact with: waiters, policemen, even the dentist working on his teeth. But after he blasted away some visitors like John the Baptist, Michal and I counseled him to turn down the flames just a smidge.

Michal used to get a kick out of how Orion would say his name with a flourish (like "Bond, James Bond"). That got me curious and we looked up the name Orion and found out it meant "the fool." This, for sure, would not do. So I found another name for him—Jair, which is translated "he enlightens." And just like that, Orion turned into Jair.

You never knew how long people would be assigned to a colony. When Jair passed through the basic courses, he was rotated to another location. Even Nathanael and Michal were shipped out and replaced as shepherds. I was sorry to see them go. As far as leaders, before Kentucky my experiences were positive. I always felt loved and cared for. So I was not prepared for what came my way when Nathanael and Michal's replacements arrived.

Our new shepherd was a short little black-haired despot by the name of Helon. The name fit him because he was *hell-on-wheels*. I don't know what possessed the Cincinnati crew to put Helon in charge of the Kentucky Farm, but I have a sneaking suspicion they wanted to get him the hell on out of their colony. He almost always wore a critical smirk on his face like he was just biding his time to rip you to pieces with his soul-shredding spiritual insights. His wife, a thin sour-faced chick, had a habit of walking around with her arms crossed as if taking mental notes of infractions to report to the KGB.

That first night they gave their introductory testimonies. Helon rattled off a brief history of his time in the Children of God, mostly focusing on his rise in the ranks to his current exalted position. Let's just say that brotherly love wasn't exactly pouring off him. His wife told the short story about how God showed her she should marry Helon, like it was a privileged status. I started to get a bad feeling in the pit of my stomach when Helon told us about his latest vision where Jesus appeared like a huge giant and, reaching down, picked up a tiny Helon to put on his lap.

"Jesus was my master and I was his pet," he proclaimed.

I wondered, *"Does he really think we're going to be lapdogs in heaven?"*

Helon was big into personal dreams, visions and revelations. This was just the first of many choice tidbits he shared for our edification. Fortunately, we didn't see much of him during the day because he spent lots of time holed up in his little leadership bus. I learned from Michal that shepherds had to do regular reports detailing what was going on in the colony, including progress notes on each member under their care. Since Helon wasn't exactly the brainy type, I can see why those reports took up most of his time. Meanwhile, I kept plugging along with my little flock of students.

The babes and I loved each other and we had a great time going through the basic classes. The Bible prophecy classes were my favorites since the end-time message was so dramatic. By now I had a whole binder filled with notes to help me chart it all out. My students were so excited to learn and loved to throw in comments and extra verses. Now it was my turn to say, "That's heavy, brother. Really heavy."

Something memorable happened when I covered the last few chapters in Revelation, the ones predicting the end of the world, the end of evil, and the creation of a new earth. When we came to the part about New Jerusalem—a magnificent city with the tree of life and water flowing from the throne of God—I was overwhelmed and felt light-headed. As I sat there staring into space, all the babes thought I was having a vision.

"Tell us what you saw! Tell us!"

"I don't think I can put it into words. But just for a moment I was filled with the awe and wonder of God's reality. My mind couldn't handle it. I almost passed out."

We all spontaneously praised God, hugged each other with delight with tears in our eyes, and rejoiced to have God's living Word.

It was a great experience: preparing classes, teaching, and loving those brothers and sisters. As I said, Helon rarely showed up during one of my classes; however, after dinner we had to endure his harangues. No one was actually misbehaving, but that didn't deter Helon. He was good at inventing nebulous accusations.

"I heard you guys laughing and the Lord gave me Proverbs 24:9—*The thought of foolishness is sin."*

It was like being rebuked by the thought police. Of course, Helon was an equal opportunity chastiser and didn't leave me out of his ESP exhortations. One night he singled me out in front of the group.

"Salem, I know you are full of pride because you're the teacher here. I can tell by your tone of voice. You think you're hot stuff, but the Lord hasn't even given you a wife yet. I have seen you looking at my wife. I know you are lusting after her."

This was going too far. I was sorry I ever laid eyes on that skinny bitch. I silently mused, *"Brother Helon, you are starting to royally piss me off."*

You may wonder why I stayed there under such a nut job. But I always tried to look at the big picture. First off, I thought Helon was an aberration. Second, I thought he was an idiot. Third, I thought the Lord would take care of him sooner or later. So, I endured it for the sake of the babes. Most of all I dreaded it when Helon met with me to have what he called *leadership training.*

During one such session Helon said, "I'm going to tell you something to see if you are ready to be a leader. Let's say a colony shepherd has to go on a trip and has to leave his wife behind. Happens all the time, right? Well, she might get lonely in bed, you know? So it might be the duty of another brother to comfort her by taking her into his bed. What do you think about that? Can you handle it?"

By now I was used to Helon's line of crap, but this was different. Was he actually promoting wife swapping? I took it as more proof that Helon was cracked.

We would go out on witnessing trips and invite people to come to visit us. Others folks just heard about our colony tucked away in the woods would stop by to chat. In Kentucky it was called *having company* (this was before cable TV and the internet). One day a young man named Raymond came by. He attended Saint Mary's Catholic seminary nearby and was very interested to hear what we were up to. After that first encounter, he returned often to fellowship. While I felt an immediate bond with Raymond, Helon—who was raised Catholic—disliked him and would mock him mercilessly for his Catholic beliefs.

But Raymond would take it all patiently and say, "Thank you, Helon, for testing my faith."

That's the oppressive leadership we suffered under. Then came the day when Helon—in one of his moods—called for a meeting. He called it a "purge session."

"The Lord has shown me that you guys are out of the spirit. I can sense you are just walking in the flesh. If that is the way you want to be, fine! So from now on there are no rules. You can all do your own thing. You don't have to do chores. You can eat whatever you want. We'll see how you like it. What are you waiting for?"

We all just sat there in stunned silence and watched as he went to the fridge, pulled out some ice cream and marched off to his bus. I went upstairs to the attic to ponder the situation. All the babes followed me and gathered around my bed with worried looks on their faces.

"Salem, what's going on? What did we do wrong? What should we do now?"

I thought for a minute and told them, "Let's just do what he says."

"But we don't want to be in the flesh."

"Let's just pretend," I said. "Then let's see what happens. After all, we're just following his instructions."

So we tromped downstairs, put on some music, ate some unauthorized snacks and spent the rest of the day "walking in the flesh" as best we could. We even went outside and played hide-and-seek like little kids.

As I suspected, that evening Helon called us together and blasted us for doing exactly what he had commanded us to do.

"I told you that you were all out of the spirit. You really proved me right."

And on and on he went. But all during his tirade I was plotting. *"That's it—you little prick! I've had enough. One of us has to go."*

Time was running out for our bad shepherd. The next day I was supposed to go out provisioning with Shaphat; so, I stayed up late and wrote a letter describing Helon's unloving behavior, his rudeness and general weirdness. I stuck it in an envelope and addressed it to the leadership in Cincinnati. I knew I was taking a risk. Would I be the one to get in hot water? Once in town I dropped the letter into mailbox with much fear and trembling.

Less than a week later two cars pulled up to the house driven by leaders from Cincinnati. As they went into Helon's bus to speak with him and his brainwashed wife, I thought, *"Now it has hit the fan."* After what seemed like a great while, they came out, followed by Helon and his wife carrying their suitcases. As they were driven away in one of the cars, Helon flashed me dagger eyes.

Then it was my turn. The driver of the other car—one of the head honchos—asked me to join him in the bus. He gave me a hug—always a good sign—and smiled.

"So Salem, you used the power of the pen to bring down the proud. We were very concerned when we got your letter and thankful you had the guts to write it. Helon has been removed...to get some more training. We have a replacement in mind, but it will take a few weeks to get him here. Can you watch over the flock till he arrives?"

And that was that. I got a short-term promotion. The days that followed were glorious. It was May and the weather was awesome. At last I could see the splendor of Kentucky in full bloom. My classes with the babes went on with renewed vigor. Our loving bond was no longer interrupted. I felt like singing, "Ding-dong the witch is dead!" In the afternoons we played baseball, touch football and occasionally hide-and-seek (our inside joke). I was just one of the guys, still sleeping in the attic.

Raymond came by and invited us to visit his Catholic seminary and meet all his friends, many on their way to becoming priests. He offered to provide lunch. So I got together a small team, all male since no girls were allowed on the campus. After the meal we had a great time—sharing our testimonies, singing songs, and describing the gypsy life of a Family member.

A few days later Raymond returned to our house with one of the fellows I met at the college. They had dinner with us and we spent quite a bit of time discussing the Bible and what the Christian life should look like. When it was time for them to leave, Raymond's companion wouldn't budge.

"I've made my mind up. I'm not leaving. I want this to be my family."

Raymond and I were speechless. But this guy was determined. So Raymond drove off alone, leaving his friend with just the clothes on his back. We named him Matthew because of his instant decision to leave his old life behind, like the tax collector in the Bible who dropped everything to follow Jesus. You would think he would have some struggles with such an abrupt decision, but as the days went by he was as happy as could be. Raymond did return with a suitcase of his clothes along with news that Matthew's parents were on the warpath.

Sure enough, a few days later his parents and older brother rolled up prepared to haul Matthew away by force if necessary. As a former greeter, I tried all my strategies to calm them down; but they were having none of it. Matthew's older brother was especially threatening. When it looked like they were actually going to grab Matthew, I shouted, "RUN!" This was a prearranged plan I set up beforehand in case things got rough. Matthew jumped up and ran like a jackrabbit into the woods before anyone could think to follow him. Matthew's mother was weeping and calling for her son to come back.

"We just want to talk to you," she cried.

But I yelled, "Don't do it!"

The father and brother were both foaming at the mouth and looked ready to beat me up. They said they were going to town to get the cops. I had to do some quick thinking.

"That is a good idea," I said. "Please bring the police. After all, the boy came to us and he is not an under-aged runaway."

Being the son of a lawyer served me well that day. The struggle was soon over and Matthew's family reluctantly left with their hopes dashed. We retrieved Matthew from his woodland hiding place; but the next day we took him to town to catch a bus to the Cincinnati colony. They took him in and he stayed with the Family for years.

As promised, Cincinnati did send in another shepherd to relieve me. But in dropping off the new guy, they also came to pick me up.

The Cincinnati leader said, "Salem, the Family is recruiting faithful brothers and sisters to go to Europe to start colonies all over the world. We think you are a good candidate. What do you say?"

What did I say? What else could I say? "Here am I, Lord. Send me."

On the drive to the Cincinnati colony, I wondered what life would be like for me in Europe. *There was no way I could foresee the radical changes coming my way.*

5

July 1972 to November 1972

The clever cat hopped up on his master's knee
And purred in his ear, "Please be content me.
If you give me some boots, a bag and some string,
I will take you to the palace of the king"

THE TRIBE OF HAM

SO WHAT WAS THE NEXT STEP in my exodus to Europe?

In Cincinnati I was given a questionnaire to fill out. Apart from the usual stuff, I had to outline where I joined, what colonies I had been at, what leaders I had served under, and all my past jobs—print shop worker, greeter, cook, babe's ranch teacher. I thought things were looking pretty good on my missionary-to-Europe resume. The next day I was ushered in to meet with the alpha dog—a clean-shaven guy with a toothpaste smile whose name I can't recall. (If I didn't write down names in my journal, they are pretty much irretrievable.) We greeted each other with a brotherly hug and then sat down on some chairs in his office. He pulled out my questionnaire and thumbed through it.

"So Salem, you were at TSC with Joab. Now he's a heavy brother, right?"

"For sure. He was my Babe's Ranch teacher."

"That must have been great."

"It was. I was there when he got the revelation about Moses David."

"Wow! That's awesome. Okay, it says here that you've been to Europe before."

"That's right. I spent a summer there learning French."

I explained that I was part of a high school group that went over to study at a French language academy. I left out the part about what I discovered when I got there: No minimum age for alcohol. Some language instruction might have accidentally worked its way into my head, but I had a busy schedule of drinking, smoking, playing poker and messing around with the female students. My high school chaperone got upset and called my father to complain about my behavior. I was kind of amused—Really? You just ratted me out to my dad who is my role model for drinking, smoking, playing poker and messing around with women. Nevertheless, when the program ended, miraculously, I could speak enough French to have a basic conversation.

I told him, "I found a French Bible and I've already memorized some verses."

"Bonus points for that. And you still have your passport, right?"

"Right."

"Brother, you are ahead of the game. Now you just need money for your plane fare."

Raising traveling money would require a trip back home to "spoil Egypt" (even more than I had already spoiled it). It was the last half of June when I called my dad and asked if I could come for a visit. He said he would have a round trip ticket waiting for me at the airport.

I had not seen my father for a year and a half. He was surprised when I got off the plane because I was pretty clean-cut and neatly dressed—not the scraggly longhaired rebel he remembered. I also ran up and gave him a big hug, something I definitely did not learn by his example. As the days went by, it slowly dawned on my father there were other changes. Before joining the Family I was a lazy, sloppy, spoiled, doped-up mess. After months of strict discipline, submission to authority, hard labor and personal sacrifice in a drug free environment, I seemed like a new creature. He liked that part of my transformation. But when he saw that I kept my Bible with me at all times and quoted salvation verses to everyone I met, he was probably thinking, *"Jesus Christ! He's worse than his mother."*

My dad was on wife number three at the time—the very woman who brought about my parents' divorce. (I think my dad racked up five or six wives during his life—but I lost count.) Anyway, this lady was definitely better suited for my father than my mother was. I met her after the divorce and she was actually a great stepmother. I liked her a lot because she was one smart and sassy lady who spoke her mind. One time her daughter—a gay rights supporter—asked her what she would say if one of her kids turned out to be gay.

My stepmother snapped, "I'd tell them: Honey, that's fine, I'll always love you. Oh, and by the way, you were adopted."

Dad was not motivated to support my mission, but he did lay some spending money on me. My stepmother was more sympathetic and slipped me some more. My cash count was about $200—still not enough for my fare to Europe. But my stepmother had a big surprise for me. She worked for a Texas airline and had access to special discount airline fares available for employees. At the end of my visit she handed me a ticket good for stand-by passage to pretty much anywhere in the world. My mind was blown!

So it seemed like I was set. After a good visit, I took a bus and swung by Houston to see my mom. She had recently remarried and was quite happy that she could finally quit all her little part-time jobs. Her new husband was a postal worker—so they weren't exactly rolling in the dough—but mom scraped together enough to buy me a new guitar. It came at a cost: I had to endure a visit from the elders of her church who tried to convince me I had joined a cult. This was the first time anyone used the C-word on me. Mom's enforcers were insistent that I should repent and return to the Church of Christ.

Before leaving, they prayed for me. "Lord, help this young man to see the truth."

Then it was my turn. "Lord, please lead these gentlemen out of the darkness and into the light."

I flew back to Cincinnati and took a bus to New York City. The cost of bus tickets, meals and various necessities shrunk my meager funds; but I finally made it to the New York colony—the Family's departure lounge for disciples leaving for Europe. While there I helped in the kitchen, taught a few Bible classes and brushed up on my French. Most folks were either raising funds for airfare or waiting for final approval. But I already had my plane ticket and my approval from leadership.

After checking out the flights, I formulated a plan: I would fly to London and then travel by train to France. I submitted this proposal to leadership and they supplied me with addresses and phone numbers. It was only a couple of weeks before I got the word.

"Pack up, Salem. Someone will take you to the airport in the morning."

"Does the London colony know I am coming?"

"Don't worry. We'll take care of that."

I knew that in order to use a standby ticket there had to be an empty seat available. When I was dropped off at the airport, I rushed to the London flight desk to get my name on the list. I thought it wouldn't hurt to get in good with the lady behind the counter.

"I'm a Christian missionary on my way to France. How's it look for standby?"

"Sorry, Hon, this flight is totally booked. It doesn't look very good. But I'll send up a prayer."

I sat there watching the clock and saying my own prayers. Then the passengers started boarding. The line dwindled down almost to the end and then my new best friend motioned my over.

"We have a no-show and you are at the top of the list."

"God was saving that seat for me," I said.

"Don't I know it," she said with a wink.

It was a very long flight and most people slept. But not me—I was too excited. They had these little headphones so you could listen to music. Right when I put them on, Don Maclean started singing *Bye, Bye Miss American Pie*. It was my first time hearing it and as I listened, tears filled my eyes. It felt like a personal message: *I caught the last plane to the coast with the Father, Son and the Holy Ghost*.

We arrived at the London Heathrow airport late at night. When it was my turn to show my passport to the British official, he asked the reason for my visit. I told him I was a tourist because that seemed better than saying I was a missionary. The guy frowned when he found out I didn't have a round trip ticket and had me stand to the side while he dealt with the other passengers in line. Then he turned to me.

"What are your plans, son?"

"I'm on my way to France."

"How much money do you have?"

"I've got 97 dollars."

"That won't get you very far, mate."

Whatever the magic money number was, I was far from it. This gatekeeper didn't know what to do with me, but I could tell he felt sorry for me, all alone and stranded like I was. I kept giving him puppy dog eyes. So he picked up his phone and called his supervisor and discussed my status. After a brief conversation he hung up the phone and said, "I can't let you in unless there's a British citizen who will receive you as a guest."

"I have an address and a telephone number."

He dialed it up. "Hello, yes...well, I'm calling from Heathrow and there's a young American who just arrived from New York City and gave me your phone number. Says he was supposed to call when he arrived. But I need to speak with a British national or we can't let him in. Right...here he is."

When I picked up the phone I heard the voice of another American. I told him my story and he said not to worry because a British brother was ready to vouch for me. And that was that. I handed the phone back and it wasn't long before my passport was stamped.

The gatekeeper smiled and said, "Your friend wasn't expecting you tonight. But all's well. He's on his way."

So I got into the UK by the hair of my chinny-chin-chin. A brother picked me up and drove me to a part of London called Bromley. On the way he informed me that no one was expecting me on that night or any other night. Someone in New York dropped the ball. It was very late at night when we arrived; but I was escorted to meet the leader—someone named Hosea—who was in his office with Sampson, the British brother who came to my rescue over the phone. They had me go over my whole story in detail—including the standby ticket and border entry.

Hosea laughed and said, "I don't know how you managed it. They don't let anyone in the country without a round trip ticket. And you only had 97 dollars? The Lord must want you here, brother."

Then they asked me all the usual questions. When and where did you join? What colonies have you been at? What kind of work I have you done? I gave them the short version, adding that I was on my way to France. They just smiled and nodded the whole time.

"So, what do I do now?"

"We'll talk about it tomorrow. Meanwhile, welcome to jolly old England."

I crashed on a big couch and awoke mid-morning, still suffering from jet lag. After breakfast, Hosea called me back into his office to meet a brother named Laban. Of course, I had to recount the whole border entry thing again, now with a few embellishments.

Then Hosea turned to Laban, "Brother Salem here worked in our Texas print shops. Don't we need some help in our print shop here?"

The London operation published a Family newspaper called *The New Nation News* and Laban was the print shop leader. I was getting the picture—France would have to wait.

In the print shop, Laban showed me how to do newspaper layout. There were no computers back then, so the secretaries typed out the story texts into narrow columns. I cut them up and used rubber cement to paste them onto a big sheet of paper. The stories and pictures were all about the Family. Mo always said, "Give them a sample, not just a sermon." In effect, the newspaper was like a big witnessing tract.

It was enjoyable being in the shop with all the illustrators and writers. As I watched them work, I had an idea. For most of my life I read comic books, graduating from Superman to Spiderman to R. Crumb. I used to draw my own comics with dreams of becoming a cartoonist. When I showed some sample drawings to Laban, he let me do the occasional illustration.

The Bromley colony was an old warehouse packed with disciples from all over Europe. The ground floor had a kitchen and a large open space used as a dining hall. The upper floor was divided into several rooms used as offices or sleeping quarters. The print shop was also up there. I found out that Sampson's father owned the place and let us use it.

PLEASE BEAR WITH ME AS I highlight a few personalities.

As I've mentioned, Mo produced four children with his first wife, Mother Eve. All four could be seen coming and going, in and out of the Bromley colony. Since Mo's sons and daughters helped kick-start the Children of God, they were treated like red-carpet celebrities.

Adults on top row, left to right: Mother Eve, Faithy, Mo, Deborah and Jethro. Adults on bottom row, left to right: Hosea and Aaron.

Mo's youngest daughter, Faithy, was a charismatic fireball. She would often lead large group meetings and give passionate speeches to motivate the troops. She could get people so roused up they might be inspired to yank out their eyeballs and give them to her if it served the cause. Faithy would take groups out to Hyde Park to win people for Jesus and recruit disciples. You would often find her playing her guitar and singing soulful songs to the lost souls. As the Children of God grew in numbers, Mo sent Faithy out to pioneer many other locations in Europe.

Mo's son, Hosea, was the one who rescued me from the Heathrow customs agent and cancelled out my plans for France. He wasn't a flashy leader like his sisters. Compared to other shepherds I had been around, Hosea seemed rather low-key—more like a behind-the-scenes guy. I never saw him lead a big meeting, but he did have quite an impact on my life (as you will see coming up pretty soon). I have a distinct memory of Hosea's voice—it was unique with kind of a twang to it. He is pictured here in Libya witnessing to Gaddafi.

I previously heard many stories about Mo's other son, Aaron. He had an encyclopedic knowledge of the Bible and could produce a vast array of memorized verses on any subject—especially when confronting skeptics. He was also well known for writing songs (although his offbeat lyrics were an acquired taste). Aaron was left-handed and had to flip a regular guitar around in order to play it.

And that only leaves Mo's other daughter, Deborah. You may recall that I met her back in Texas. She was slender and had long blond hair. Some found Deborah intimidating, with a bearing that commanded attention as she *strode* through the colony. Together with her husband Jethro, they had a bundle of kids. Deborah's role had expanded since her days of running that small school at the TSC colony. She was now in charge of the Family's childcare ministry and had set up a bigger school somewhere near Bromley. One time I heard her rebuking a young man who was not doing a job up to her high expectations. I wasn't on the receiving end, but I was cowed. When she was out of earshot, an older brother whispered to me, "Now that's what I call pussy power."

After 17 months in the Family, I had beefed up a bit and my hair was longer. It was quaint being in London, but colony life was pretty much the same. Once again I found myself in a dorm room filled with bunk beds and brothers. Apart from my main job in the print shop, I was also assigned plenty of other chores. So, I didn't have much down time. Everyone drank a hell of a lot of tea—something I never got the taste for. For snacks they would spread this disgusting brown concoction called Marmite onto bread. I tried it once and had to spit it out.

We had this big red double decker bus for witnessing trips. Everyone called it the Prophet Bus. When we went to Hyde Park, we always put on a Holy Ghost Sample—same deal as in the USA—with the usual singing and dancing and skits. When I noticed they still used the old impromptu Randy skit, I had a brainstorm and asked to see Hosea when we returned home.

"Do you think I could try writing a new skit for the park? I took drama in high school and performed in several plays."

Hosea said, "Okay, brother...let's see what you've got."

My first attempt was just a variation of the Randy Skit—but I tweaked it by adding an extra part...Satan! When something bad happened to Randy, Satan appeared by his side to tempt him with negative thoughts. I, of course, took the part of the devil and threw myself into it. My partner in crime, a dear brother named Peter Piper, played Randy and was equally dramatic as he triumphantly received Jesus and rebuked Satan. Then I would shriek loudly and slither away.

Here I am in Hyde Park in my role as the Devil.

After the performance Hosea asked to meet with us in the Prophet Bus. He said, "Well, boys, that was quite a show. Do you think you could come up with another script? And Salem? Maybe tone down the Devil part, okay?"

So that was the start of a little drama ministry I called *The Tribe of Ham* (having a bit of fun with the Family's old tribal system). We would frequently take the Prophet Bus to parks and music fairs to mingle with the many young people passing through London. I would strain my brain coming up with new ideas for short plays with a message. Here is one of my first scripts. (I actually discovered it on a tattered piece of paper folded inside one of my journals.)

The Freezing Man

Lost Soul: (shivering) I'm freezing to death. I've got to find a way to get warm.

(Rich Man enters wearing a tie and holding cash)

Rich Man: What's the matter with you, young man?
Lost Soul: I'm so cold. Can you help me?
Rich Man: Why son, I know just what you need.
Lost Soul: You do? What is it?
Rich Man: Money! Spending money always makes me feel good.
Lost Soul: But I don't have any money.
Rich Man: No money? How sad. But here, I'll let you borrow some of mine. (counts out 10 bills and gives to Lost Soul) Of course, you'll have to pay me back...with interest.
Lost Soul: (still shivering with handful of money) What's interest?
Rich Man: It's why I'm interested in loaning you some money.
Lost Soul: But I'm still cold.
Rich Man: You'll feel better if you buy something. Let me sell you this tie.
Lost Soul: Okay, if you say so. How much for the tie?
Rich Man: It costs 10.
Lost Soul: (counts out 10 and puts on tie) I'm still cold.
Rich Man: But you sure are looking good. By the way, I need my interest payment.
Lost Soul: I spent all my money.
Rich Man: Then I'll have to take your tie. (takes tie and exits)
Lost Soul: (shivering) I'm still freezing. What can I do?

(Teacher enters with books)

Teacher: Let me help you. I'm a teacher. Listen to this poem:
Great is the sun, and wide he goes
Through empty heaven with repose;
And in the blue and glowing days
More thick than rain he showers his rays.

	Doesn't that just warm your heart?
Lost Soul:	It's nice. But I'm still cold.
Teacher:	Some people never appreciate the finer things in life. (exit)

(Radical enters with signs)

Lost Soul:	I'm so cold. Can you help me get warm?
Radical:	Comrade, what you need is to join the movement. We're all hot radicals.
Lost Soul:	What do I have to do?
Radical:	Here, hold this sign and let me teach you how to chant. *What do we want? Change! When do we want it? Now!* (Both march and chant)
Lost Soul:	I'm still cold.
Radical:	But now you have plans and dreams. (starts chanting) *Plans and Dreams! Plans and Dreams!* (Both march around chanting)
Lost Soul:	Excuse me. I'm still freezing. When will I start to get warm?
Radical:	Can't take it, eh? The revolution isn't for sissies. (yanks sign away and exits)

(Jesus enters wearing a jacket)

Jesus:	I've been looking for you. I can see you're freezing to death.
Lost Soul:	I am. I've tried money, education and revolution. I'm still cold.
Jesus:	Those things will never keep you warm. Here, my jacket will protect you from the cold.
Lost Soul:	How much does it cost?
Jesus:	I've already paid for it. All you have to do is let me put it on you.
Lost Soul:	That's all? Who are you?
Jesus:	I'm Jesus.
Lost Soul:	(hold out arms) Jesus, please help me. If I don't get warm, I'll die. I need to be covered by your jacket.
Jesus:	(puts jacket on Lost Soul) That will save you from freezing.
Lost Soul:	How can I ever thank you?
Jesus:	You could help me find other freezing people.
Lost Soul:	Lots of my friends are freezing. I can't wait to tell them the good news.
Jesus:	Let's go. (both exit)

This script became kind of like a Swiss Army knife—I could use the same format but change it around as needed. For example, instead of *The Freezing Man*, it could be *The Starving Man*—who finally got the Bread of Life from Jesus. I could also jazz it up with other characters, like a meditation guru, drug pusher, or a preacher. Peter and I got a lot of mileage out it.

THE BROMLEY COLONY WAS LOCATED in South East London.

The school Deborah set up was within walking distance just a few miles away on Chinbrook Road. One of the teachers there was a sister everyone called Rebecca Red because of her long, flowing scarlet hair. I met her when we were out witnessing and she asked me if I would consider coming to the school to do a little play for the kids. I told her that I could do better than that—I could put on a magic show. So we set a date and—as could be expected—it was a huge hit with the children. Afterwards, Rebecca gave me a tour of the school. She explained that they used the Montessori method—Deborah's inspiration—and demonstrated some of the colorful equipment. I was quite impressed.

I still worked at the print shop, but I was sometimes pulled away to write and organize drama productions at parks and music fairs. I also dressed up as a clown and put on more magic shows as a way to witness to children. Each one of my tricks delivered a spiritual message.

I visited the school whenever I had a chance. It fascinated me. Okay. Maybe pretty Rebecca Red fascinated me as well. They always needed extra help to watch the children during meals or on the playground. Since all the teachers were female, the children loved having a guy around. Even after I found out that Rebecca Red was already married, I still looked forward to being at the school.

I would occasionally see Deborah at the school. Her oldest son, John, was there and he was what my mother used to call "a ring-tailed tooter."

One day I had the kids outside for recess and a teacher told me to bring them in. I told John playtime was over, but he refused to listen.

He proclaimed, "I don't have to do what you say. You can't spank me!"

He had me there. So I said, "I can't spank you, but I can hold you down."

I grabbed him and held him tight so he couldn't move. After some struggling he finally surrendered, "Okay! Okay! I'll go in." (These days I'd probably get thrown in jail for that.)

One afternoon Deborah approached me and said, "I've been watching you with the children and I think you are very good with them. Have you ever thought about being a part of the childcare ministry?"

"Uh... hmm... I'll pray about it."

Just a note here—when you said you'd pray about something, it could have different subtle interpretations. Saying it with enthusiasm (*I WILL pray about it!*) indicated you liked the idea. Saying it with hesitation (*Well...I'll have to PRAY about it*) usually meant you weren't convinced. Many times the phrase was a polite stalling tactic.

Of course I said I'd pray about it because, after all, this was Deborah asking. At the same time, I had a different idea about my future. Hold your horses. *It's true I have a great time playing with the children... but to do it full-time? I don't like the sound of that.*

As I said, at that time all the childcare workers were women. That part didn't bother me. But they worked behind the scenes and you didn't see much of them. Not my style. I wanted to serve God in a big way, to be a heavy brother, perhaps even the shepherd of a colony. I wanted to be in on the action—certainly not on the sidelines babysitting. What I really wanted was to spearhead a drama ministry for Jesus and travel around the world performing. *A star is born, baby!*

But Deborah's recruitment talk didn't scare me away from the school. The children were happy every time I showed up. They certainly were interesting creatures, like little sponges, constantly soaking up information into their databases. I loved reading them stories, really making it dramatic for them. They would sit cross-legged around me and follow my every word, laughing with delight at the funny parts and asking me a million questions after the story ended. That was the start of a slow tug on my heart. As time went by, I looked forward to my time with the children more and more.

Meanwhile, I was getting cozy with an artist at the print shop named Miriam (pictured here in Laban's lap, clowning around with the other artists) …

She had long brown hair and a beautiful smile. As we got to know each other, Miriam expressed an interest in being in one of my little skits. I readily agreed because we didn't have a regular female player for our productions. It wasn't long before Miriam joined Peter Piper and me during our occasional outings. As time passed—and I'm sure you won't be surprised here—I began looking at her more and more fondly. But I kept my little crush to myself. Or so I thought.

Peter and I were on laundry duty one day and he came across Miriam's bag of dirty clothes. He rummaged around inside and pulled out one of her bras, draped it across his chest and said, "Oh, Salem…these are just for you."

I laughed, "Very funny, Peter."

"Come on, Salem. Shouldn't you practice undoing the fasteners on this bra?"

"What are you talking about?"

"Don't give me that," he said, "It's obvious what's going through your head."

I was surprised at Peter's discernment, especially since I thought I was playing it cool.

Was it that obvious? Had Miriam picked up on it? Maybe that wasn't a bad thing. Could it be that Miriam was just waiting for me to take the initiative?

A SHORT TIME LATER THE whole Bromley colony started buzzing with activity. I didn't know what was going on, but I could feel the vibes— lots of brothers and sisters arriving from other colonies and hush-hush meetings going on. Then someone announced Deborah was to be crowned the queen during a big coronation ceremony. We didn't know what that meant, but it sounded exciting. I was asked to prepare a special little skit to perform at the coronation, so I got to work on it. Meanwhile, the downstairs of the Bromley colony was decorated like a royal dining hall, complete with a red carpet and throne.

On the night of the coronation the dining hall was packed. Then in came the leaders, all dressed up like Lords and Ladies of the royal court. I don't know where they got the costumes for this, but it was like out of an old movie. When everyone was seated, Deborah appeared, decked out in a queenly gown. Big Josh—one of the London leaders—wore a royal chamberlain outfit and followed her carrying a crown on a velvet pillow. A hush fell over the crowd as Deborah sat on the throne. Big Josh gave a flowery speech and with great pomp placed the crown on Deborah's head. Then the musicians started playing "God Save the Queen" and everyone rose to their feet cheering and singing.

After the coronation, big bowls of punch were brought out. Now this was real punch—English style and spiked—so it really packed a punch. I had not touched a drop of alcohol since joining the Family, so this was extraordinary. The musicians started played familiar tunes and there was the usual singing, clapping and dancing in the Spirit. At last it came time for my little skit—I guess that made me the court jester. Here is the script for the performance Peter and I put on that evening:

Tickets to Heaven

(Enter Mr. Works—a salesman in a flashy suit.)

Come one, come all—both big and small
Wait until you hear about this—an offer you don't want to miss
But you need to act fast—and get it while it lasts
It's genuine, it's sanctified—it's bona-fide and that's no lie
It's a hundred percent guaranteed—to be exactly what you need
It don't matter who you are—where you're from, near or far
Skinny, fat, brunette, blonde—from a big or little pond.
No matter what's messing up your day—this will chase your blues away
Does your liver quiver?—Does your heart smart?
Are you feeling run down? —Life's giving you the run around?
Are you washed out, freaked out—flipped out, pooped out?
You may have problems galore—but I have what you're looking for
This is it, your lucky seven—I am selling tickets to heaven
Don't be shy, step up, be bold—or you might miss those streets of gold
What does it take to buy cloud nine—just what is the bottom line?
I won't lie. There is a price—to get all the way up to paradise
Now don't you fret, all isn't lost—we've worked hard to lower the cost
But I must tell you before I'm done—this offer is not for everyone
If you want to classify—your goodness rating must be high
And if your record ain't so great—you'll have to pay an increased rate
But lying scoundrels, thieving skunks—shameless whores and stinking drunks
Real bad girls and bad guys, too—these tickets are absolutely not for you

(Enter Mr. Grace, waving a big handful of tickets.)

Mr. Grace:	(shouting) Free tickets to Heaven. I've got free tickets to Heaven!
Mr. Works:	Hold on! What did you say?
Mr. Grace:	I said (shouting) Free tickets to Heaven. I've got free tickets to Heaven!
Mr. Works:	That's crazy. You can't just give away tickets to Heaven. Why, what if some dirty, rotten sinner gets one?
Mr. Grace:	But these tickets are for the lost, the ones Jesus preached to.

Mr. Works:	Are you insinuating that Jesus associated with sinners?
Mr. Grace:	Of course. Jesus died to save sinners.
Mr. Works:	(gasps) How dare you say that. Besides, you're ruining my business.
	You better stop or I'll have to use force.
Mr. Grace:	But I can't stop telling everyone about the good news.
Mr. Works:	You asked for it. (grabs Mr. Grace and threatens with clinched fist)
	Aren't you going to fight back?
Mr. Grace:	Nope.
Mr. Works:	Don't you understand? I'm going to punch your lights out.
Mr. Grace:	Go ahead. I've already got my free ticket.
Mr. Works:	You mean you really believe the tickets are free?
Mr. Grace:	Absolutely.
Mr. Works:	And you don't have to pay for these tickets?
Mr. Grace:	Jesus already paid for them.
Mr. Works:	And they are for everyone?
Mr. Grace:	Yep. You just have to have the faith to take one.
Mr. Works:	Even me? To be honest, I can be a rascal.
Mr. Grace:	Even you.
Mr. Works:	(takes a ticket) Wow! This is amazing. This is good news. Thank you.
Mr. Grace:	Don't thank me. Jesus did all the work.
Mr. Works:	Could you use any help passing out these tickets?
Mr. Grace:	That would be a great way to say "Thank You Jesus."

(Both exit, shouting, "Free tickets to Heaven!"

Our performance was received with great enthusiasm (bolstered by the punch, I'm sure). Afterwards, I saw brothers and sisters making their way up to Deborah to say a few words. Seemed like the thing to do, so I got in line. When I reached Deborah, she smiled and told me how much she enjoyed the skit.

Then she touched my arm and said, "Salem, we are moving the school to a different location. We could really use your help since you already know the children."

"I'd be happy to help with that. I love being with the children."

"Have you thought more about joining the childcare ministry like we talked about?"

"Yes, Deborah. I'm trying to make up my mind."

She gave me a look. "Okay, let's talk about it. Soon."

DID ANYONE HAVE QUALMS ABOUT a woman ruling over us?

I'm not sure how the other top leaders felt, but all of us peasants were thrilled with the idea of having a queen, even if we didn't understand the political ramifications (those were matters on a shelf out of our reach). Besides, we all knew that Mo orchestrated the event. And sure enough, it wasn't long before Mo sent out an announcement to all the colonies around the world:

> "In accordance with prayer and prophetic vision, the King's Firstborn, Deborah, was crowned Queen of our new Revolutionary Kingdom Government of God's New Nation by Archbishop Joshua in an extremely dramatic and colorful ceremony on September 21, 1972, the Fall Solstice, with other princes, princesses and beautifully costumed lords and ladies in attendance rendering due homage and pledging their loyalty and faithful service to our young Queen Designate and God's chosen Royal Family and ordained elders. It is regretted that not all the Royal Family were able to be in attendance...including the Queen's diligent, loyal and faithful Prime Minister, Jethro, who continues to head the Queen's Government as administrator of Her Majesty's business affairs, Exchequer and diplomatic relations, and to whom we trust you will give your utmost cooperation!"

Did you catch that? *Royal Family?* That was a new one. In later communications Mo made it clear that he and his blood relations—his four children, their spouses and the children they produced—were to be honored as being of *royal blood*. It was just another layer to our communal fairy tale. The extraordinary had become ordinary. We thought our group was so exciting we should make a movie about it.

Meanwhile, the pressure was building for me to make a decision. I loved performing our shows in the park. That was my witnessing technique. But then there were the children. If I taught them about the Bible and Jesus, wasn't that like witnessing?

I also felt a burden about Miriam. How could I pop the question? So I came up with a little scheme. I wrote a short play about a boy and girl progressing from friendship to romance. Then I asked Miriam to read it and give me her review. Miriam was happy to give me her opinion about my writings (Miriam was always willing to give you her opinion). I sat there all nervous as she read it. I could tell she was a bit puzzled, probably wondering when I would get to the part about Jesus. But that never came. The last lines went like this:

Boy: I enjoyed being with you today.
Girl: Yes. I had a good time.
Boy: It kind of makes me wonder.
Girl: About what?
Boy: About us being together.
Girl: Do you mean what I think?
Boy: I think we make a great couple. How about it?
Girl: What are you trying to say?
Boy: Should we get married?
Girl: _____

At the end. Miriam looked up. "You didn't finish it. You left out the girl's answer."

"Miriam, that's for you to write. How about it? Should we get married?"

She stared back down at the script for a while, gathering her thoughts. Then she carefully folded the pages and handed them back to me.

"I'll pray about it," she said.

Miriam on our magazine cover

It wasn't the answer I hoped for, but it wasn't a "no." Miriam and I continued to see each other quite a bit. No doubt about it, I thought Miriam was the gal for me. And I prayed about it—prayed that Miriam would see the light. As much as we hung out, I guess it was inevitable that others saw us as a couple. A few weeks later Miriam and I were sitting together in the dining hall when Big Josh came over and knelt down beside our table.

"Behold! What is happening here? Two of God's little plants beginning to intertwine their vines?"

After Josh left there was an uncomfortable silence. So I changed the subject and we didn't discuss it any further. But alarm bells went off in my head. Sure enough, a few days later Miriam asked for a private moment.

"Salem, I have been praying about us and I'm sorry—I think God has someone else for me."

Miriam turned me down and for sure, it bruised my pride. What? She wasn't hot for me? I wasn't used to being romantically rejected. Before joining the Family I had several girlfriends and for the most part they did the flirting, pursuing and even seducing. That gave me the impression— like most young bucks—that I was quite charming. To learn that my allure had limits was a revelation for poor little Salem. But I comforted myself by looking at it spiritually—*God closed that door*. (When things didn't work out as expected we would call it a "Closed Door.")

Meanwhile, the publishing department experimented with a different publication—a little magazine that was called *The New Improved Truth*. I was really impressed when the first issue came out. They had a guy who was great with an airbrush and the front page was dazzling. Soon a witnessing trip was organized so we could distribute copies. But this time Jethro instructed us to sell the newspaper! As far as I can recall, this was the first time the Children of God sold any literature. But at that point, I think it was just an experimental exercise.

I stood outside a London underground station—the tube—and hustled the commuters as they walked down the long inclined walkway. I walked backwards next to my potential customer, held out a copy of the paper and flashed a winsome smile. If they stopped, I had a line ready to use.

"Your gift will support our work with troubled youth on drugs."

Ten pence—the asking price—was a handy coin most Londoners carried around. As can be expected, I was turned down a lot; but when it was time to return home, my newspapers were gone and my pockets bulged with coins. It was a blast.

Tick, tock... I still had to give Deborah an answer. Would working with children be a good fit for me? Since it was a big decision. I asked to meet with Hosea.

I explained, "I'm trying to decide what my ministry should be. I'm working in the print shop, but I would like to start a drama ministry. And now Deborah wants me to consider working full-time with the children."

Hosea was quick in his response to my quandary. "Well, as far as the print shop goes, more people are coming from America. We can easily find someone to take your place. When it comes to the drama ministry, I don't think it's a full-time job. If I were you, I would seriously consider Deborah's offer."

It came to me later that Hosea's sister, Deborah, might have put a bug in his ear about me. Nevertheless, his counsel was enough to nudge me in the direction of children. What eventually helped me make a final decision was the realization that whatever meager talents I had could be useful with the children—my love for drama and art would not be lost. The next time I saw Deborah I told her I finally made up my mind. She was very excited and told me to move to the school so I could help pack it up. In a few weeks the school would be relocating to a house in northwest London.

I was not looking forward to telling Peter Piper about the change. We had grown close. My sense of humor matched very well with his. Jesus said you should never say "Racca" to anyone (being interpreted, "Thou Fool!"). Peter and I loved that word and used to trade versions of how exactly we would say "Racca" to another person. I still remember the offensive faces and ugly voices Peter would come up—it had me in stitches. I knew Peter would be bummed out when I told him about my decision. Peter was an underappreciated loner, but had finally found something to connect with (drama) and someone who got him (me). Leaving my friend behind left a hole in my heart.

We rushed to pack the school material into boxes and load them into vans for the move. Once at the new location, a fairly large house in Hampstead, I helped with the unloading and unpacking. While the teachers set up the classrooms, I would often be in charge of a group of children. When all the work was complete, I asked what was the next step for me. Deborah told me I could take classes at a Montessori Training Center in London.

As I walked around the school after dinner one evening, the classrooms were dark and peaceful. I was happy with my decision and looked forward to my new ministry. Just then I was jarred out of my pleasant meditations by a sister with an urgent message.

"Someone is calling you from Texas."

Oh no, I thought, what could this be about? It was my father.

"I've been trying to reach you for days. You must get home as soon as you can."

"But why, Dad?"

"You've been drafted into the Army."

6

December 1972 to May 1973

The maid looked down at Tom. "Oh proud fellow," said she
"I think in a mouse-trap much safer you will be"
So she picked up Tom Thumb and shut the lad up tight
There he was held captive for many days and nights

PRISONER OF WAR

BEING INDUCTED INTO THE ARMY was not part of my life plan.
I should have seen it coming; but since I was one of God's soldiers, I expected the angel of death to pass over me. When I dropped out of college in Austin I became eligible for the draft. Back at the Kentucky colony I got a notice to report for classification. That involved filling out paperwork, walking around half naked with a bunch of other guys, and being poked and prodded by doctors. All through the process, even in my underwear, I was busy passing out tracts and witnessing.

When some officers walked by, I did not waste the opportunity.

"Do you know Jesus? He saved me from my sins and made me a new creature."

They stopped. One of them said, "We get one of these nut jobs in here occasionally."

They walked away laughing; but I kept it up as I was shuffled around. Later one of the doctors checking my eyes whispered, "I heard you witnessing and I've been praying for you."

I was classified 1-A (cannon fodder) and my name went into the Selective Service lottery. When I was called for duty, the summons bounced around with no response. Finally, the draft board contacted my dad with this message: *If your son doesn't get his ass to an induction center, he will be prosecuted as a draft dodger.* During our dramatic phone conversation, my father urged me to get home as soon as possible.

I went to see Hosea and asked, "Should I just ignore all this draft business?"

"No Salem, you can't do that. We believe in obeying the laws of the land."

"Does that mean I'm the lucky winner of an all-expense-paid trip to Vietnam?"

"Not necessarily. A lawyer could help you get conscientious objector status.

So I packed up and flew back to the States to meet my fate. While I had never participated in the anti-war marches that were going on, the Vietnam War did trouble me. Was it a fight for the right? Unlike America's involvement in World War Two, I didn't see a clear-cut rationale. And there was no way I could accept "Ours is not to reason why." My high school argument went something like this: *I don't want to be like those German soldiers who said they were just obeying orders when they machine-gunned the Jews.*

However, I had a different line of thinking now. I was a disciple of the Prince of Peace who famously said, "If my Kingdom were of this world, then my servants would fight; but my Kingdom is not of this world." How could I desert my calling to fight in a worldly war, especially a morally questionable one?

After a long series of flights back to Texas, my father picked me up at the airport. On the drive to his house we stopped off at his law office to have a chat.

"Son, you have a hearing at the draft board tomorrow. What will you do?"

"Dad, my religious convictions will not allow me to participate in fighting."

He sat back and stared out the window. "I had a feeling you would say that. What about a non-combat position?"

"But wouldn't that still be supporting the war?"

He leaned in close and looked in my eyes. "Would you go to prison for your beliefs? That's a possibility, you know."

"If it comes to that, I have no choice. I'll have to choose prison."

My father was a war veteran and I knew he despised draft dodgers. I expected fireworks, but to my everlasting amazement, he gave me a pat and said he would personally represent me at my hearing. To this day I can't quite fit that into my brain. My father, the man's man and teller of war stories, would stand up for me—the son he could not fit into his brain.

The next day we went to the local draft board. I spoke to a small panel about my beliefs. One lady, who looked like she could do lots of Army pushups, repeated my father's question about prison. I gave the same answer. At the end my father stood up.

"I fought in the War and I never believed the people who claimed to be conscientious objectors. I just thought they were cowards. But I know my son is sincere. If there ever was a conscientious objector, he is the genuine article."

I just sat there, speechless and tearful. My daddy. The meeting adjourned and my case was kicked up to a higher authority. This was the beginning of a waiting game. The army axe was poised over my neck.

I stayed at my father's house for two months while my case rattled through the system. During that time I worked in a little downtown magic shop. The owner was delighted to have a helper who actually knew how to demonstrate the magic apparatus. As for me, it was a blast to fine tune my sleight of hand skills.

In January a peace agreement was reached between North and South Vietnam that would end the United States involvement in the War. Later it was announced that no further draft orders would be issued. It sounded promising, but I had already been drafted. So would it help me? While we waited for the draft board's final decision, my father said I was free to leave as long as I remained in Texas.

I was still tethered, but on a longer leash. My next stop was a place near Grapeland, Texas—the Family's USA headquarters. Everyone called it the "Selah Colony." I still don't know why. The word "Selah" is found in the Book of Psalms and nobody really knows what it means. But it became one of the Family's special lingo words meaning "something secret." For example, we would say, *"Don't share this with your parents… it's SELAH!"* Anyway, it was located in an old school. The man that owned the property loved the Family and let them have run of the place. It was a fairly large colony with several travel trailers and mobile homes scattered about.

I thought I had landed in clover when I learned that Cephas, the one who first coaxed me into the Family, ran the operation. The place was packed with leaders, but my good buddy Cephas was the *capo dei capi* (boss of the bosses).

Someone in England had videotaped the entire coronation, including my skit, and copies were sent for everyone to see. It didn't take long for word to get around that I was the guy in the skit giving a royal performance. I got asked lots of questions. What was it like? What is Deborah like? And like an idiot, I had plenty of tales to tell of my hilarious antics overseas. But I discovered things were much different at the Selah colony. Mo had recently written about the judgments about to fall on America. In this somber atmosphere, it was like, *"Hey, we don't have time to mess around."* It took me a while to adjust.

Before I left England, Deborah told me the Selah colony had a school for their kids. When Cephas heard about my interest in childcare, he sent me there. The school was located on a small farm out in the country with cows and chickens. A dozen or so children were boarded there during the week. At first it seemed so idyllic, like a very nice place to be (Bwah ha ha! Cue the VILLAGE OF THE DAMNED music score).

MY FIRST NIGHT THERE I was asked to give my testimony.

This was the standard operating procedure when you went to a new place. I gave them the expected rundown: my salvation story, where and when I joined, and the leaders I worked under—all the usual stuff. But then I went off script and recounted my more exciting experiences. Doing skits before hundreds of people. Performing at the coronation. Blessed by Deborah to work with children. I just rolled along with my lively rendition, blithely ignoring the tiny alarms going off in my head. It seems my testimony got some tongues clicking. The leaders at the school came to one conclusion: This guy is LIFTED UP.

In the Family "lifted up" and "puffed up" were synonyms meaning proud or arrogant. This was high on the naughty list. As I knew full well, if a leader thought you were proud, you were in for some serious verbal bitch slapping. It was right up there with the sin of complaining, also known as "murmuring". We all dreaded hearing our superiors say, "Is that a murmur coming out of your mouth, brother?" But to have a leader lampoon you with "Pride goeth before a destruction" was far worse.

The main leader of the farm and school complex was a guy named Noah. His wife—a thin blond chick with the face of an elf—was the power behind his throne. Her name escapes me, so I'll just call her Mrs. Bossy Pants. Then there was the head teacher, Lebanah (also blond, but full-figured). She dished out wisdom to her little band of teacher trainees. So these three—Noah, Mrs. Bossy Pants and Lebanah—were in charge of my re-education camp. When it came to Salem, they all had a bug up their collective ass. I was weighed in the balance and found lacking humility. What is the duty of every good leader when dealing with a proud disciple? *Take him down!*

Since being humbled was supposed to be good for the soul, I guessed it was my turn for a blessing. Still, it was a tough transition. You see, in England I was the funny guy, the guy who organized all the skits, the guy who Queen Deborah herself had personally recruited for the childcare ministry. I had talents. I was appreciated. But I had been yanked from Tim Burton's colorful Batman movie and shifted into Christopher Nolan's gritty one. My personality, the one that worked for me so well in England, did not play well in the dark universe. I soon learned to hide my personality and construct a new one in order to survive the gauntlet. The order of the day was STIFLE.

I was actually the first male childcare worker in the Family. Perhaps Lebanah thought I would invade her feminist domain. In the classroom she instructed me to sit on the sidelines and just watch. (*"Do nothing to distract the children."*) This wasn't easy because I was a novelty. Since the kids were accustomed to female teachers, they were curious about this guy sitting there.

"Who are you? What are you doing here? My name is Sammy. What is your name? Come see what I'm doing. Can I sit in your lap?"

I felt like whispering out of the side of my mouth, "Beat it, kid. You're gonna get me busted."

Lebanah was always shooing the children away from me (I could almost see her feline tail puffing out). Hey, there wasn't much I could do about it. But still, it was fun sitting there and I actually learned a lot by watching the action. After class I started reading all the Montessori books. When the kids were in bed, I spent time in the classroom practicing with the Montessori materials.

Outside of the classroom, Lebanah was pleased to delegate certain jobs to me: serving the children lunch, putting them down for naps, watching them play outside, and getting the bed-wetters up in the middle of the night for a trip to the potty. That was fine with me. I was determined to be a lowly nun, no matter how menial the task. But it made no difference—Lebanah criticized everything I did with the children.

"Salem, Salem. You're not performing in one of your plays anymore. You simply must learn to control your mannerisms. Montessori teachers model appropriate behavior for the children: our posture, the way we speak, even the way we walk."

"The way we walk?"

"Yes. When you walk into a room it's like you're making a grand entrance. You need to tone it down." (Apparently, in Texas, I couldn't even walk right.)

Mr. Bossy Pants—I mean, Noah—was kind of a control freak with schedules and reports. And no surprise, he liked lecturing you about your faults and failings. Thankfully, he was away from the school quite a bit, over at the Selah colony (probably turning in his reports and getting lectured about his faults and failings). Each night everyone at the school had to turn in a Tribe Report—a small piece of paper we filled out describing our day. We did Tribe Reports in Kentucky and they only took a few minutes to fill out. But Noah redesigned them to his specifications and gave us a list of questions to answer. (l) Did you learn any lessons today? (2) Did you have any battles? (3) Did you read any Bible chapters? (4) Did you memorize any verses? (5) Did you read any Mo Letters? (6) How much sleep did you get? (7) Did you get any exercise?

I have to say, Noah was a minor irritant compared to his wife, Mrs. Bossy Pants. She was my main tormenter. In her mind I was a misfit who required discipline. She would get on my case for all kinds of things, mostly chicken-shit stuff. I got in trouble for having a certain look on my face. If I sang a song, I was singing "out of the Spirit." Ah, yes! Being "out of the Spirit" was one of her favorite accusations. It was so handy and nebulous. Once I accidentally walked through the room when she was having a meeting with the sisters in the colony. You can guess what Mrs. Bossy Pants told me later. "You were in the flesh when you walked through the room." (Note: "In the flesh" and "out of the Spirit" were synonyms.) If something I did really irritated her, she would rat me out to her husband. That meant a summons to their trailer for an exhortation. I had landed in *One Flew Over The Cuckoo's Nest* and Nurse Ratched was out to get me.

Things were not looking good for poor Salem. Lebanah did not express great confidence in my teaching potential. ("Are you sure the childcare ministry is right for you?") Mrs. Bossy Pants seemed to think I was a hopeless case. My heart was heavy and I wondered about my future. Did I make a mistake going into childcare? Meanwhile, my draft case was not resolved. Was prison still a possibility? After three months of this I was in a gloomy state.

Journal Entry (March 23, 1973) Maybe I should give up the idea of working with children. Yesterday I prayed that the Lord show me how I should serve Him. I took a blank sheet of paper and prayed, "Lord, this is my life. I want you to fill it in." Then I signed the paper at the bottom and promised that I would follow His directions. I then burned the paper as a sacrifice of faith.

A few days later I received a letter from Miriam in England and was stunned by what she wrote: *I've been praying about it and maybe it is the Lord's will for us to get married.* What? Didn't we settle that? Didn't she already turn me down? I wrote her back: *No thanks!*

Meanwhile, the rebukes came in on a regular basis. "Getting rebuked" was Family lingo for when leaders chewed you out ("Because we love you"). By this time I was afraid to open my mouth and say anything. Except for my bizarre experience with Helon in Kentucky, I had been happy with leadership. However, these guys in Texas were seriously screwing with me. They didn't seem wacky, like Helon, so I started accepting their message: *Bad dog, Salem.* I didn't feel loved (or even liked). During those months my journal entries were filled with dreary introspection.

Journal Entry (April 5, 1973) God have mercy on me and help me to be humble and learn my lesson. Damn the devil and his doubts. I'm sick of them!

At the end of April I came down with the same kind ailment I had back at the Merkel colony. Like before, my throat looked horrible. In case I was contagious, they put me out in a small camper trailer by myself. The general consensus was that the Lord sent the illness to teach me the error of my ways.

"Pray about it, Salem. God must have something he wants to teach you."

I'm sure they had a clear idea of what I should hear from God. I was secluded for over a week, away from the constant barrage of criticism. So I did pray and took some time to really think things over. It came to me that in England I had no problem being myself with the children, kidding around with them and enjoying their quirky way of looking at things. That's what got Deborah to notice me in the first place. So, what's going on around here?

Did I make mistakes? Sure. Did I need to be humbled? No doubt. But did I deserve all the flak thrown at me? Was I really such a hopeless screw-up?

Hmm...here's a thought...maybe not.

As I pondered my recent history, a little picture came to me. It's like I had smooth sailing until a storm threatened to wreck my plans. I could give up or launch out once again. I was surprised when it all came together in the form of a poem.

THE BROKEN VESSEL

Walking by the restless sea
I saw a ship approaching me
I climbed aboard and in the hold
I found a book with leaves of gold
The words made my longing heart yearn
To be on the craft when it returned
So I could serve on the other side

Across the ocean's great divide
With peace of mind I was inclined
To launch the ship leaving all behind

But as it traveled homeward bound
There came an ominous thunder sound
A storm raged on and lightning flashed
I saw the rocks and felt the crash
The humbled sails no longer soared
A broken vessel returned to shore
The sand beneath my feet exclaimed
Why not give up? What have you gained?

But as I wavered, book in hand
It fell and opened on the sand
The pages cried out in unity
Faith and Love will set you free
My fear fled away and I gave a shout
Though sails are tattered I'll not doubt
And then the wind was turned about
The sea arose, turned inside out
And I, the book, the boat and sea
Were at the place prepared for me

Perhaps this whole Texas deal was a test of my faith. After all, hadn't God guided me towards working with children? Then an idea popped into my head. *"I just need to stick it out until I can get the hell out of here."* I decided that when I returned to the general population I would keep this revelation to myself. (My little secret. Selah, baby!) If only I could get back to Europe. But I would have to be clear of the draft problem. I would also need clearance from leadership (and not much hope getting it from these guys). So I prayed earnestly for a solution.

When my throat cleared up, I returned to regular duties. But now I had some hope. I also had a humble role to play—the new improved Salem. It worked. Lebanah told me my sickness had changed my attitude (damn right). Even Mr. and Mrs. Bossy Pants cut me some slack.

In the next few weeks some dramatic things took place. First, I received notification from the draft board that I was reclassified as I-H, meaning my draft situation was cleared up. A huge burden lifted off me. Then—BAM!—I received another letter from Miriam.

"Mother Eve thinks we would make a good match. She is going to speak to Deborah about getting you back to Europe."

Wow! What an interesting development. After all, I needed some higher authority to free me from my captors. So I wrote a letter to Deborah asking if I could return and work in her school. To give it a little more pizzazz, I included my new poem, explaining that I received it while praying about my ministry.

Journal Entry (April 13, 1973) Last night we all went to the main colony for a big meeting. Cephas told us that Aaron died while doing some mountain climbing. Then everyone shared memories about him.

Meanwhile, as if things weren't already bleak enough around this place, Mo pumped up the anxiety level. He hinted that Nixon might take over the government as a dictator (and called him "Nitler"). Mo declared that America was the "Whore of Babylon"—as mentioned in the book of Revelation—and ordered the publications department whip up a special tract with the drawing of the whore with her legs spread. A highway led up between her thighs and a city landscape sprouted from her crotch. At Mo's insistence, these were mailed to everyone on our mailing list—including our parents. Yikes!

Journal Entry (April 25, 1973) I got a letter from Deborah. She said she loved my poem and really wants me to come back to Europe. But she's not in England anymore. Now she is in Italy. She said she would contact the leaders here to work it out.

Sure enough, the Texas leadership soon got word that my presence was required in Italy. That was an official clearance from Queen Deborah herself. My drama critics took the news with poker faces. What could they say? Six days later I left the school to catch a bus.

Back at my father's house, I asked him for the money required to enroll in the Montessori Training Program—quite a sum when you included the cost of the books on the reading list. To my surprise, my dad was all for it. In his mind this was a positive step because I would actually receive a teaching certificate. He wrote me a check for the tuition and I mailed it off to England.

But I still needed cash, especially considering my last experience upon entering England. So I toured all my old stomping grounds in Houston with a beggar's cup extended. Things went surprisingly well and my fund-raising thermometer registered higher and higher.

Before I left town my mother urged me to call my old girlfriend, Barbi. She probably hoped Barbi would coax me out of the family. This was ironic because when I graduated from high school my mother was afraid that Barbi and I were rushing into marriage. But now it might be a way to get me out of the cult.

Barbi had long dark raven hair and a voluptuous figure. (And yes, when she signed her name she put a heart over the i.) I had written Barbi several times, trying to get her to join the Family. No luck with that. Anyway, Barbi was very happy to get my call and said she'd come right over. Hmm…mom was at work and I was alone in the house. Did it occur to me this was risky business? Perhaps a brief warning flash was sent to my brain. But being such a strong disciple and all, I disregarded it.

I heard her car in the driveway and opened the door. As soon as I saw Barbi in the flesh, all was lost. Muscle memory flooded in and I stopped thinking with the head on my shoulders. We wound up on the couch and I rounded the bases headed for a homerun. But as we worked on buttons and zippers, that pesky Jiminy Cricket whispered in my ear. I froze and started to pull back.

But Barbi just pulled me closer. "Don't stop now. Make love to me."

"I'm sorry. I have to stop. It's against what I believe now."

"But why?"

"I can't. I just can't.

"But you started it."

"I know. It was wrong. Please forgive me."

Barbi pushed me away and started crying. Then she stood up, buttoned up and wiped away her tears.

"You've changed. You're not the guy I knew before. And I don't like this new person."

I tried sharing some Bible verses with her—mostly an attempt to reconstruct my righteousness—but I'm sure they sounded hollow. Barbi drove away and out of my life, leaving me shocked at how quickly temptation crumbled my celibate purity. Was I that much of a pushover? Yes I was. No doubt, this would take some serious repenting.

The next day, very much disgusted with myself, I formulated my travel plans. I discovered it was cheaper to fly to Paris and go by train to Italy. I never told anyone about my close encounter with Barbi. I was counting on a more holy future.

If I only knew what was coming my way.

7

May 1973 to October 1973

The witch gave the children candy to eat
And soon the hungry pair went fast asleep
When they woke up from their sugary nap
They found they were locked inside a trap

THE CHILDREN'S HOUSE

I PLANNED TO SPEND A day in Paris before leaving for Italy.

This time I had no problem getting through customs. So I was feeling pretty good as I used my very rudimentary French to catch a bus to the Paris colony on 17 Rue Ursins. When I knocked, a French girl opened the door.

"*Bonjour.*"

"*Bonjour. Je suis...* how do you say... American. Do you speak English?"

"*Un Americain? Oui!* I speak a little English."

"And I speak a little French."

"*Comment t'appelles-tu?* What is your name?"

"*Je m'appelle Salem.*"

"My name is Tirzah. Do you know Jesus, Salem?"

"*Bien sûr...* of course." Then I gave her the Family's three-finger salute.

"Oh! You are one of us? *C'est bon! Entrez.* Come in."

"*Merci*, Tirzah."

"*Bienvenue ici.* You are welcome here. But why are you in Paris?"

"I'm on my way to Italy."

She took me by the elbow and introduced me around. After many hugs and hearty greetings, she led me to a crowded room where people sat on the floor talking.

"Are you hungry? Yes? Wait here. I will bring you food."

I was in the middle of telling my story for the second time when she returned and put a plate next to me. When I reached out for it, someone walked by and accidentally stepped in the middle of the plate. I looked up and got a shock. It was Miriam! I never expected to see her in Paris. All the letters she wrote me were from England.

She stared down with a very red face. "What are you doing here?"

I stared up. "What are you doing here? I thought you were still in London."

"No, Faithy recruited me and...well...you know how she can get you fired up. So, here I am. Hold on. I'll get you another plate."

By the time she returned, the leader of the colony had arrived to check me out. He was a genuine French dude with long blond hair and a beard. Everyone called him French Joseph. (Having names with your nationality was a practice that faded away as more Europeans joined the Family.) Anyway, he told me about some big leader who recently passed through France. It was hard for me to focus on his story because my mind was racing after seeing Miriam.

I asked myself, *"Did God engineer this serendipitous encounter?"* Back in London Miriam rejected my initial proposal—and that stung—but then she wrote me about having second thoughts. I responded with a rejection letter. And now our paths crossed unexpectedly in Paris. Very interesting.

Someone loaned me a train schedule and I found one departing for Italy the next day. I didn't have much time, but wanted to clear the air with Miriam. I found her in the kitchen.

"Can we take a walk?" I asked.

"Sure. I'm really done in here."

As we strolled along the Paris streets, I told Miriam my nutty Texas story. Then she told me about her departure from England and gave me a rundown of the Paris colony. Miriam had a rather low opinion of French Joseph; she described him as a little Napoleon who jettisoned his first wife for a newer model. He pissed Miriam off and one night—to show her disdain—she filled out her Tribe Report on toilet paper. I had to admit, that was impressive.

Then Miriam stopped and gave me a look.

"Salem, isn't it funny? Us being thrown together like this? Me being here and you just happen to show up."

"Yes, Miriam. I think it's a strange coincidence."

We didn't settle anything; but just like that, Miriam was back on my list.

AFTER A LONG RIDE I arrived at the train station in Florence. I was jet-lagged and sleep deprived, but still had a ways to go. My final destination was the small town of Certaldo. I looked around for a train going there, but couldn't find one. Now what? My French would not get me very far. Then I noticed a small kiosk with a sign that said "INFORMATION." That's just what I needed. So I walked over to speak with the lady behind the counter.

"Do you speak English?"

"Yes. Do you need help?"

"I sure do. I need to get to Certaldo."

"I am happy to help you."

She flipped through the pages of a booklet.

"I think it is best to catch the bus. The cost is not great. Is that good for you?"

"Yes! Thank you."

She wrote down the number of the bus and gave me directions to the bus station. Thankfully, it was within walking distance.

Certaldo

The bus was packed when we started out. But after a lengthy ride with many stops I was the only passenger left when we arrived in Certaldo. I showed the colony address to a few Italian folks who used many hand gestures to direct me to a dirt road. As I trudged along with my backpack, guitar and a suitcase full of Montessori books, the road seemed to go on forever. Sweaty and exhausted, I finally came upon a huge villa and knocked on the front door. Once inside I walked in on a birthday celebration. There were lots of familiar faces—Deborah, Jethro (the birthday boy) and many of the kids I took care of in England.

The villa was like something you saw in a travel brochure. A genuine Italian nobleman named Emmanuel had married a sister in the Family named Rachel. Rachel, a stunning beauty, would have been hard for any man to resist. As a result, Emmanuel let the Family use some of the buildings on his estate.

When the party ended, a group of us walked down another dirt road to a peasant cottage not too far away. The cottage—also known as the "Bassetto School"—was a quaint, two-story stone building with rustic roof tiles. After the children were shuffled off to bed, I crashed on one of the classroom floors.

The Bessetto School

When I got up in the morning the house was quiet. I walked out the front door and saw children in the yard very focused on some sort of industry. They had gone into a neighboring field and plucked handfuls of wheat. As I watched, they used a couple of stones to pound the grain into powder. Then the leader of the pack licked her finger, dipped it into the flour and sucked on it. The others followed her example and ran to get more wheat. As I strolled around the property I could see we were smack dab in the middle of a vineyard. Next to the school was a field of wheat. The roads were lined with rows of olive trees. I had been transported to Eden.

Just then someone called my name. I turned and was greeted by Sarah Ireland—the head of the school. She said, "So you're the one Deborah told me about."

I didn't know what to make of that, but it sounded promising. Sarah—an Irish lassie—was pleasingly plump and spoke with the expected brogue.

"Let's get you some breakfast and then we can have a chin wag."

Sarah was quite the talker and caught me up on all the local goings-on. Likewise, it didn't take long for her to wring out my life story. After that I got the tour of the building and grounds.

There were several rooms upstairs. Two rooms had bunk beds for the children stacked three high (never saw that before). Three rooms were used as classrooms: one for the toddlers, one for the preschoolers and one for elementary students. The classrooms were filled with the same colorful materials I had seen before. The other rooms were used for staff bedrooms. On the ground floor there was a kitchen and a large dining room complete with a built-in pizza oven. Mama Mia!

Sarah said, "I'm so happy you're here. We really are quite short-handed. So I hope you're ready to get to work."

"Well, I only just started my Montessori course."

"Oh, don't be worrying about that, Salem. Consider yourself in training."

I was excited to learn about the Family's approach to education. I knew Maria Montessori set up her first experimental school in the slums of Rome back in 1906, calling it Casa dei Bambini—the Children's House. The street children she serviced ranged in age from two to seven years. But it worked. The children were allowed to pick the work they were interested in with no pressure. I didn't know how all this freedom stuff worked, but it sounded great.

At first Sarah split my time between the preschool and elementary classes so the kids could get used to a new person around. It didn't take them long. And unlike my previous experience in Texas, Sarah didn't have a problem with children crowding around me. In fact, she was determined to give me teaching duties as soon as possible. That meant special training sessions after the children were in bed at night. When I mastered a certain set of material, Sarah had me practice with the children the very next day. I was tossed right into the action.

"If Deborah brought you here, you must have the right stuff."

Sarah's husband, Demetrius, was a bushy-bearded American who usually wore overalls. He wasn't the boss of anyone—more like the school handyman with a little tool shed out back where he could whip out shelves or tables for the classroom. There was another couple at the school: Ezrom and Cedar. Cedar was a secretary and Ezrom was a jack-of-all-trades around the estate. Ezrom was a familiar face because he had arrived at TSC just a few weeks after I did. I remember him coming into the Babe's Ranch with a big smile and this huge mass of curly black hair down to his shoulders. Ezrom and Cedar slept in an old bus parked at the back of the school. I hung out with Ezrom and Demetrius in my spare time and entertained them with magic tricks and old Lenny Bruce routines.

Emmanuel's estate was like a leadership hub and print center. There was also a Babe's Ranch in a separate building on the other side of the estate. The Bassetto School was a place where parents on the estate sent their children to board from Monday to Friday. It was almost like homeschooling. The kids would get picked up for weekends; but since everything was within walking distance, we saw lots of parents during the week when they had free time. Each school night I put a foam mattress down in the middle of my new bedroom—the elementary classroom.

It turned out that Deborah's hidden agenda was to stick me with the older kids—kindergarten age and up. The preschool and toddler classes were well staffed, but Sarah was the only one who could handle the older kids. However, she was constantly pulled in many directions. Apart from her teaching duties, she also trained the teachers and ran the school. On top of that, Deborah wanted Sarah's help to develop an International Childcare Ministry for the Family.

There was a slight problem with this plan. In the elementary class Sarah was like a strict but loving mother. The kids listened to her. She was the female alpha dog and all their little tails drooped down in her presence. It is often assumed that children will have more respect with a male teacher, but whenever Sarah was called away and I was left alone with the children, their tails raised up like flags. "Fresh meat. Yum! Looks tasty."

Bassetto School (June 10, 1973) The children behave for Sarah but not me. I don't know what to do with them. How can I teach them when I need to be taught?

One weekend I went out with a group to an Italian beach. My job was to watch three of Deborah's children. Things were going well until Little Joy, Deborah's oldest daughter, started giving me a hard time. She was either 9 or 10 years old at the time, but was nevertheless a pistol-packing pre-teen. It wasn't long before Little Joy disappeared. I was pretty frantic, but couldn't leave the other children to search for her. She returned hours later, feeling quite cocky about the whole incident.

When we got back to the school, her father, Jethro, got wind of the rebellion and had me watch while he scolded his daughter and gave her a few whacks with a belt. To his credit, Jethro showed no anger. The spanking was short and far from excessive. When Little Joy left, Jethro turned his attention to me.

"My kids can sense weakness like a shark smells blood in the water. If you don't show them you're the boss, they will eat you up."

I guess it was a nice way of saying: *My children need limits and you're a softie.* He probably pictured me bound and gagged with a bonfire at my feet while his little savages ran wild. But was he telling me to whack their butts if need be? As a child, I got my share of spankings—mostly by my mother using a thin little belt she kept in the kitchen drawer—but I couldn't picture myself marching around the classroom with a big stick.

Still, I needed to get the kids' respect. What to do? What to do? I decided it was time for some good, old-fashioned *Psychological Warfare*.

PSYOPS Strategy #1: Take Down the Big Chief

Little Joy—who considered it cruel and unusual punishment to be in the classroom with younger kids—was definitely the leader of the resistance. And now I was on her shit list for getting her busted. That was unfortunate because I was actually quite fond of her. Hoping my scheme would work, I called her aside.

"Little Joy, I want you to be in charge of checking everyone's work. Make sure the kids are not messing around."

I could see the wheels turning in her head, not quite convinced; so I had to sweeten the deal.

"Here, you can use my pen."

You see, pens were just for the teachers. The children only used pencils. So that was my bag of magic beans to coax her—the pen of power. Soon she relished her new post. It also brought her out of her shell. Previously slouching around and sullen, Little Joy started to show a different side. She put up with the younger kids with patience and gentleness. Little Joy was becoming a joy—no longer too cool for school.

PSYOPS Strategy #2: Establish Soft Power

By this time I was familiar with the children's work—at least what they were supposed to be working on. And the kids had a fair amount of freedom. For example, if they liked to read, they could focus on that first and save math or writing for later. There were no assigned seats; they could choose where to work (most of them ended up on the floor). But during work time the children did not have the freedom to play around or disrupt others. Of course, that was exactly what a couple of them wanted to do, especially since they had a stupid new teacher.

I tried taking the most outrageous offenders aside, hoping my rational pleading would inspire a noble response. Okay…that proved futile. Time for a new approach. One morning I started the class with a meeting. I placed a single chair to the side of the classroom and said, "This is the watching chair. If you can't make good choices, I will take away your freedom. You can sit in this chair and watch the others doing good work."

Of course, five-year-old Philip (another offspring of Deborah and Jethro) immediately tested the system by running around the room and generally bugging everyone.

I said, "If you choose to break the rules, you are choosing to spend time in the watching chair. Go sit down and I will talk to you about it later."

"NO! I'm not going to sit in that chair." He stomped away.

"Philip, until you sit in the chair, you have lost your freedom. Do not touch anything in the room or talk to the other children because they are working."

Philip fumed for a while, but (amazingly) didn't try to get things from the shelves or interact with the other children. After a few minutes I heard some scraping noises and looked up to see that he had removed the watching chair and replaced it with a chair of his own choosing. He gave me a look that communicated clearly: *Fine—I'm sitting—but not in your damn chair.* I let him have that little accommodation.

After several minutes he said, "Aren't we going to talk about it."

"Well, I'm busy here. I'll see you in a bit."

I made him sweat it out. After we talked it out, I released him on parole. Believe me, all eyes were on this episode. The watching chair served me well. But certain repeat offenders needed it taken to the next level. To them I delivered a different message.

"If you waste your work time I will waste your play time."

They were later shocked when I made them spend recess cleaning the classroom.

PSYOPS Strategy #3: The Play Is The Thing

When I was a kid I spent most of my free time playing outside doing all the dangerous stuff kids aren't allowed to do anymore. Could I give my little elementary crew a similar experience? Why not? So I gave them plenty of time to play and explore. In fact, I took as many lessons outside as possible. That worked out great when it came to science experiments.

But it was an epiphany when we studied history. We didn't just study early humans—we became early humans. We made mud huts, built fires, constructed stone altars and best of all we manufactured WEAPONS: slingshots, spears, bows and arrows.

Whenever possible I supported the children's fantasy play—pretty easy with old sheets and clothes they could use to make tents and costumes. Demetrius always had some spare lumber laying around for the kids to saw and hammer into interesting structures. At some point a thoughtful outsider donated some playground structures—monkey bars, a roundabout and swings. But the kids mainly used them as backgrounds for their imaginary world. In the long run, that manufactured stuff couldn't compete with just rocks, sticks and old cardboard boxes. One day a dump truck arrived and unloaded a huge pile of sand. That became the center of activity for weeks.

Another form of play was drama. Because of my background I could always get the kids' attention by reading them a story. Then the children would want to act it out during recess. That brought back fond memories of my sister and I putting on little plays for our parents. So I wrote some skits for the children to perform. They were wildly enthusiastic. And something magical happened during the process—the kids and I bonded. I can't remember hearing anyone say, "I'm bored."

As I progressed with my Montessori studies, I was surprised that no one at the school—not even my mentor, Sarah—had any training at the elementary level. So my Montessori learning curve was steeper than expected. But we did have all of Maria Montessori's elementary level books translated from the Italian (not exactly summer beach reading, by the way). So after the children were in bed, I would puzzle over her instructions. I knew all the answers were there; I just had to play catch up.

As I'm sure you have gathered, Sarah—my new "shepherdess"—was a friendly, chatty, down to earth type. We got along well and it was balm for my battered soul. I may have suffered under a few poor leaders, but I still believed that most shepherds in the Family were like Sarah. She and I would often sit around to discuss the children. After several weeks she gave me a confidence boost.

"You're kind of a natural with the children, Salem… sort of cheeky, but they love it."

My face turned red. What was this strange thing...a complement? After my recent experience, I didn't quite know how to handle praise. Would it give me a swelled head? Back at the school in Texas—under the thought police—I had learned the art of suppressing my more gregarious nature lest I be labeled "lifted up." Was it safe to emerge from my protective shell? Part of me remained on alert; but around the children, I never had to worry about a scolding for being *out of the spirit*. Kids got me. They loved that I was dramatic and playful. I felt safe with them.

OUR DRAMA PRODUCTIONS WERE A big hit with the parents.

After one of the plays, Jethro's memory was jogged.

"Salem, didn't you used to do skits for the Family back in England?"

"Yes. That was before Deborah drafted me into the childcare ministry."

"She's good at that. But now that you're here, why not put together some shows for the Babe's Ranch? You could write some with spiritual lessons. The babes would enjoy it."

"That would be fun. But I'd have to enlist some more adults."

So the "Tribe of Ham" was back in action. I put my head together with a brother named Fortunatus, who was a leader at the Babe's Ranch. Soon we put on special presentations for the new Italian converts. I often had to use an Italian translator, but whenever possible I would learn my lines in Italian (that was the beginning of my language course).

Fortunatus was one of the most happy-go-lucky guys you could ever hope to meet. He was American, but looked like an Italian with dark hair and olive skin. He was also one of those naturally beefy fellows—solid muscle from head to toe. One night at the school, with all the new disciples invited over for inspiration, Fortunatus said he had an idea for a skit.

"Okay, you know the song 'Ya Gotta Be a Baby To Go To Heaven?' So what about this? While everyone sings that song, in walks this guy wearing a diaper…like a baby, see? And then the baby does stuff to show how a new Christian is like a babe in the Spirit. Get it?"

"Yeah, Fortunatus. I get it. But who's going to wear the diaper? You? 'Cause, I'm not."

"Sure, I'll do it."

Problem was we didn't know anything about diapers. I went and asked Sarah Ireland to lend her expertise. After a while she arrived with a big white towel and the largest safety pin she could find. So far, so good…let the diapering commence. Then Fortunatus took off his pants. If I had been drinking something, I would have choked on it.

"Dude, you don't believe in underwear?"

"No, man…gotta let everything breathe down there."

Now in that area "down there," Fortunatus was well named. When he lay down naked, Sarah shot me a look of disbelief. Would it all fit inside the diaper? I hyperventilated with laughter as Sarah wrapped up that bundle of joy.

"You missed a bit there, Sarah."

Sarah gave me a smirk. "Next time you're on diaper duty, Salem."

On most weekends, with the children gone, we would go out in pairs to witness in nearby cities—out on Saturday morning and back on Sunday evening. The Family had started distributing more tracts and Family newspapers as an evangelizing tool. It worked well when combined with personal witnessing. Some people gave donations for the literature, especially after hearing our pitch, but it wasn't strict at first— we always gave Sheepy people a break if they had no cash. (*Sheepy* was a word the Family used to describe a receptive person. Sheep listened. Goats did not.) But now we started passing out Mo Letters and things changed. We were instructed to make literature distribution our main focus and to ALWAYS ask for a donation. Eventually this style of witnessing came to be known as *litnessing* (remember that for later…it's important).

When Deborah and Jethro were busy on weekends, they called upon me to take their three older children out and about. With time my role changed from teacher to nanny. Travel by train was easy in Italy and the children and I got to visit lots of beautiful places. A ride through Italy was a feast for your eyes; the sculpted fields, hills and gardens made it seem like a fairyland. The kids and I had this funny game we played on the trains to pass the time. We invented pretend languages and had animated conversations using elaborate gestures and facial expressions. The Italians had no idea they were overhearing nonsensical babbling.

One afternoon Deborah came to the school for a visit. She lined up her children and asked them to sing a song. As they started up, I could tell the kids were doing a half-ass job. All of a sudden Deborah swooped in and swatted them right and left. Man, was Deborah ever on a mission. It was hit and miss—mostly due to the children's stop-drop-and-roll reflex.

Deborah shouted, "My father taught us that our whole lives are a performance. Whenever you sing about the Lord, you better shine. Now start over!"

With tears flowing down their cheeks, the kids sang with great gusto. I watched the whole thing in stunned silence, like when you drive by a car accident. This was the first and only time I ever saw Deborah strike a child, but it was enough to freak me out.

I knew the Family used some Bible verses to justify spanking. However, I was the new guy and reluctant to use corporal punishment. But sadly, as the days went by I witnessed the other childcare workers doling out swats—some more than others—and it began to seem normal...even expected. So—full disclosure—it wasn't long before I did the same. And despite my good intentions, I'm sure I whacked a few butts unnecessarily. I loved those children and they loved me back. How could I have done that? When I think back, every spanking I gave is like a heavy stone tied around my neck.

"SALEM, HAVE YOU THOUGHT ABOUT getting married?"

I suppose it was inevitable that Sarah would ask me that question, especially after she saw me getting friendly with Eloth, a cute little sister assigned to assist me in the elementary classroom. Hey, I was twenty years old and had been celibate for over two years. In those days you were a candidate if you were female and could speak in tongues.

When I told Sarah about Miriam—our on-again-off-again history and how we ran into each other in Paris—she got a knowing look on her face.

"Quite a coincidence her being in Paris, eh? Do you think it's God's will for you to be with her?"

"I don't know, Sarah. For now we're just praying about it."

"Hmm…praying about it, are you? Sometimes you have to get off your knees to get results, you know."

Bassetto School (August 1, 1973) I got another letter from Miriam. I still think about us getting together. But now I'm wondering if Eloth is the one for me. We get along well and I love her revolutionary spirit. Eloth or Miriam? Miriam or Eloth? God, please prepare the heart of the person I will marry.

At the end of August I went out on a road trip with a new brother from Malta named Beno. Beno had a very round head, deep set eyes that slanted down at the corners, and a wide mouth with thick lips. He was a bit chunky, with a little double chin, and was always laughing and joking around. We spent a whole week riding the trains and hitchhiking through Italy, passing out literature as we went along. When it came to donations, Beno wasn't an enthusiastic salesman. I did my best, but with train tickets and food expense, we ended up in Cinque Terra with only a few lire—not enough for a hostel. No problem. We slept on the beach. But you can't eat sand.

Beno said, "Let's be beggars like Saint Francis."

"Okay. I saw a panetteria earlier. Let's go."

Since Beno spoke no Italian, I took over as we entered the bread shop. I did have some basic conversational skills because you had to learn certain Italian phrases in order to sell literature. I had also picked up a lot by memorizing lines for skits.

"Ciao. Siamo Cristiani. Ma niente soldi. Puoi aiutarci con… cibo?"

(Hello. We are Christians. But no money. Can you help us with… food?)

The baker was impressed with my meager Italian. Next thing I know the whole staff gathered around listening curiously.

The baker gave us an impish smile and said, *"Bene, bene. Ma prima canti una canzone, per favore."*

(Good, good. But first sing a song, please.)

Singing for our supper, I got it. I conferred with my partner.

"Beno, do you know any songs in Italian?"

"No. But I know how to sing The Lord's Prayer in English."

"Hey. That is not an easy song to sing."

"Sorry, Salem. That's all I've got."

So we stood there and gave it our best effort. I'm sure it was a sad performance because Beno pretty much croaked like a frog. But when we finished all the bakery staff laughed and clapped enthusiastically. We were rewarded with a loaf of bread as big as a backpack. It tasted divine, like manna from heaven.

The next night—almost fainting with hunger—we went to a restaurant to provision something to eat. The owner, a lady named Angelina, spoke some English and was very amused that we would actually ask for a free meal.

"So what you do? You go here and there to beg?"

"We are Christian missionaries going out to tell people about Jesus. We believe God will take care of us."

"Ah, Gesú. You are like the birds and come to my tree to eat. Come sit down and talk."

Since we arrived at the tail end of the day, the restaurant was not very busy. Angelina sat with us and heard both of our testimonies. Then she snapped at one of her waiters (actually one of her many sons) and gave instructions for a meal to be prepared. Beno and I were dumbfounded as course after course arrived. But Angelina never left the table, taking pleasure in our obvious enjoyment. All the time she kept talking, telling us about her family. By the time we were done it was late at night and the restaurant was closing. Angelina asked us where we were staying.

"We've been sleeping on the beach."

"No, no! Gesú has something better for his little birds."

She took us to a small room above the restaurant where we could take a bath and crash for a night. After our travels we really needed a good wash. The next morning we began our travels back to Certaldo.

Along the way Beno said, "Her name was Angelina. Maybe she was really an angel sent to take care of us. What if we went back some day and there was no restaurant run by Angelina?"

Back in Certaldo I returned to my busy life at the school. While I rarely got a break during the day, most mornings I took a walk down the road between the vineyards in order to pray. It energized me for my work in the classroom. The children continued to be lovable and hilariously entertaining (when they weren't causing my head to explode with frustration). The school was a sort of PR showpiece for the Family. We had frequent visitors who were given a tour by Rachel and Emmanuel. Although it interrupted our schedule, we considered it a part of our witness—a sample of our way of life.

My glorious first summer in Italy drew to a close. The childcare ministry I had first rejected turned out to be tailor-made for me. And I loved Italy. It was great fun to interact with all the brothers and sisters working on Emmanuel's estate, especially the Italians at the Babe's Ranch.

Rachel and Emmanuel

So what if I slaved away night and day with the kids? I was on a mission. So what if I shared a bathroom with a house full of grownups and children? I had endured outhouses. So what if I slept on a foam mattress on the classroom floor? That's better than sleeping in a room with 20 other guys. I was a young zealot and didn't think much about my personal space. What was I going to do? Decorate a bedroom with pictures and knickknacks like a systemite? Hell, no! It was a temporary world. It was all going to burn.

Was I a heavy brother at last? Maybe so if you asked one of the kids I looked after like a faithful sheepdog.

WHEN I TURNED 21 I had been in the Family almost 3 years.

All in all the good outweighed the bad. Did I ever get down? Sure. Some days I felt super spiritual, victorious, and invincible. Other days I'd wake up and didn't feel like singing another stupid praise song. But we were taught that the devil, always up to his old tricks, was especially fond of attacking the revolutionary followers of Jesus. So, whenever I got bummed out, I recited my Bible verses to reconnect with the vision. And I'd always record the victory in my journal.

David Berg was our rabbi and we followed him like the disciples followed Jesus. But—big difference—we knew Mo was just a man. Mo had no problem admitting that he made mistakes and got depressed at times. We loved him for that. Unlike other whacko religious gurus we heard about, Mo never said he was divine, never claimed to be an angel or the second coming of Jesus or some kind of miracle worker. But he did allege he was a prophet inspired by God. That was okay with us; we had read our Bibles; we knew God's prophets were not perfect. They were known to complain about stuff and even rebel at times. And since we were all TOTALLY convinced Jesus was coming back soon, it made sense that God would send an END-TIME prophet to guide us through the coming years of TRIBULATION.

I'm sure it's hard for outsiders to get our connection to David Berg's writings; however, we embraced them. *"Mo loves us and wants us to learn from his experiences so we can serve God better."* Moses, our spiritual father, even signed his letters "DAD." I won't even try to summarize his teachings—that would be an overwhelming labyrinth of a task. But one thing for sure, Mo gave us what we wanted to hear:

> *"Churches don't have the answer. God is looking for laborers to evangelize the world. You are part of a special Family. We all gave up our lives for Jesus and yes...sometimes it's hard. But it will be worth it in the end. You will have treasure in heaven. This is serious business because TIME IS SHORT."*

This is what our critics (our enemies) called BRAINWASHING. But we were willing participants; we wanted our brains washed. No one held a gun to our heads.

Something else about the Mo Letters—they were a form of Family entertainment. We didn't have television or radio—that would have been considered WORLDLY. But Mo gave us pep talks and told us interesting stories. He also talked about world news quite a bit (at least his official version). So when a new Mo Letter arrived, the colony leader would get us all together, especially if it introduced a "heavy" new idea. It was an event to be enjoyed with others—like passing around a joint. We all shared the same head-trip.

We were Hansel and Gretel nibbling away at Mo's gingerbread house. Very tasty to hungry children—but we had no idea about what was about to emerge from inside. Few of us were prepared for the revelatory bombs about to be dropped.

The first explosion came in a Mo Letter entitled *SHINERS OR SHAMERS*. Mo was not happy about the amount of his literature being distributed. He wanted to shift our focus from personal witnessing to selling Mo Letters ("litnessing"). For a group based on evangelizing, it was quite a shock when we read these words:

I can do my own preaching. I don't need you to do it for me. All I need is sweet, bright-eyed happy kids to get it into their hands. Stop this personal witnessing and just be the delivery boy. I think I can preach a better sermon than you can. You are not supposed to be preachers, just paperboys to deliver my wonder working words.

If you sold a lot of Mo Letters you were in a special category—A SHINER! If you didn't sell much, you were A SHAMER! At first the letters chosen for distribution were what we called MILKY, meaning that they were inspirational and not radical. With time this would change. Abandoning personal witnessing was a profound redirection; but as usual, we gave Mo the benefit of the doubt. After all, he was our spiritual father. And for many of us, that's what we longed for—a father to love and guide us.

Selling literature was an acquired skill. It took some trial and error. The trick was to get people to take a Mo Letter. I used to walk up to someone on the street and go, *"Sei Italiano?" (Are you Italian?)*

They would stop, always so helpful, expecting me to ask for directions. *"Si sono Italiano." (Yes, I'm Italian.)*

I would hand them a Mo Letter and say, *"Questo è per te!" (This is for you.)*

Then I would ask for a contribution to help OUR WORK. What work was that?

"We are full-time missionaries. Helping young folks get off drugs. Setting up Christian schools."

Different Family members had different methods. Some stood on a corner and played the guitar while their partner hit the crowd with the literature. Since I often had children to take care of, I would take them with me to litness. The kids would run around with the Mo Letters and collect donations. They had to endure pats on the head and getting their cheeks pinched Italian style *("Che carino!")*. But on the bright side, they might score a free ice cream cone.

Around this time Italy experienced a coin shortage. The little shops and cafes were rarely able to give change. Instead they put little dishes of candy on the counter so you could take your change in sweets. But after a day of selling lit, our pockets were bursting with the 100 lira coins the merchants were desperate for. If we went into a bar and said, "Ho spiccioli" (I have change), we got our coins swapped for bills along with a free cappuccino.

A short time later, while we were still adjusting to the new litnessing mandate, we received another Mo Letter blast called OLD BOTTLES. The title was actually another bit of insider Family lingo that takes some explanation (sorry)."Old bottle" is a term taken from the King James

Version of the Bible where Jesus said, "If you put new wine into old bottles, the bottles will break, spilling the wine. You must put new wine into new bottles." "Bottle" was the old English word for a "wineskin." So in the Family an "old bottle" was someone who had a hard time accepting new doctrine (new wine). Of course, we all wanted to be "new bottles."

Mo was giving us a signal that his letter contained a new revelation that might "break some bottles" We soon found out why. Mo now claimed his writings were more important for us to read than the Bible. In fact, he basically said we could stop reading the Bible because it was out of date. What? We were all saturated with memory verses and most of our Bibles were falling apart from use. Even the previous Mo Letters—which, admittedly, had always presented a radical type of Christianity—still quoted Bible verses for support. We all thought the Bible was the foundation of our movement. But now Mo was calling his letters "God's Word for today." It gave me serious whiplash and—for sure—my bottle was shattered.

> **Journal Entry (October 1, 1973) Rachel came down to read us a Mo Letter that was tough to hear. Mo said some things that seem wrong. He seems to be glorifying himself and honoring his words over the Bible. It is like when Jesus told his disciples, "You must eat my flesh and drink my blood." And they said to Jesus, "This is a hard saying." But the disciples had nowhere else to go. That's the way I feel.**

I hoped we didn't have to broadcast this revelation to the general public.

"Hey, guess what? You can forget about the old Bible. We have a guy who is writing a new one."

That would have really boosted our reputation—and it's not like the whole world loved and respected Mo to begin with. A whole parent group called FreeCOG was organized to convince Family members that David Berg was a false prophet. Other more aggressive parents hired deprogrammers to kidnap their children and talk some sense into them.

There was also a television news program, Chronolog, that had aired a nasty expose about the Children of God where ex-members were interviewed who said some shocking things about David Berg's supposed sexual misconduct. None of that bothered us because we had on our special true-believer sunglasses. After all, Jesus had been accused of all kinds of things. Why would it be any different for Mo? To our way of thinking, persecution was a good sign. It indicated we were doing something right.

But this scrapping of the Bible was a serious issue for me. I could accept that the Mo Letters were important—obviously more than I previously thought—but the Bible was my treasure, my joy, my comfort, my strength, my anti-depressant, and my bulletproof vest. How could I do without it? I couldn't. So I went underground. Away from prying eyes,

I kept on reading and memorizing Scripture.

But I was soon distracted from such quandaries. Very distracted.

Journal Entry (October 7, 1973) God really blew my mind this morning. I was cooking breakfast for the children and Sarah ran in all excited and yelled, "Guess who's here?" Then in walked Miriam. My stomach hit my throat.

Sarah, the matchmaker, took over my breakfast duties while I gave Miriam a tour of the school. Miriam had used her credentials as an artist to come work with the publications crew here in Italy. So after breakfast, she returned to the main house where the print ship was located and where she would work and sleep.

Upon her arrival Miriam ceased being some hazy possibility I wrote about in my journal. Didn't we agree to "pray about" getting married? Now here she was. And no doubt about it, Miriam had a lot going for her. She was intelligent, creative, outgoing and had a wonderful sense of humor. Besides that, she was downright sexy. In France the brothers called her "Sexy American Girl." But best of all, when she shared her testimony—during which she would always start crying—her love for the Lord was plain to see.

I saw Miriam often because, like the other disciples on the estate, she would come to the school for meetings. She had travelled all the way to Italy, but now she confused me. Some times she seemed happy to see me. Other times it was like I was invisible. Strangely, despite no clear signals from Miriam, my feelings for her grew. Thoughts and anxieties about Miriam filled my journal pages. Figuring her out was like trying to capture a grasshopper—when I got close she would take to flight.

In the Family marriage was supposed to move you to a higher spiritual level, getting you ready for leadership. Love was important, but it wasn't enough. You had to determine God's will. If you had God's blessing, then love would follow. I wanted to look back and think: *We love each other so much. I thank the Lord for putting us together.* But how to find the will of God was the puzzle.

Family members were always saying, "The Lord showed me this" or "God told me that." It was a big deal for us. I constantly recorded personal revelations in my journal. All new disciples were given a class about finding God's will. The main points were sung in little ditty that still buzzes in my brain: *The Seven Ways to Know the Will of God*.

Do you know the seven ways to know the will of God?
By the Word,
The Voice of the Word,
Direct revelation,
Godly counsel,
Circumstances and conditions,
By burdens,
And last of all by fleeces.

Please bear with me as I unpack it for you. It reveals how our minds worked.

(1) BY THE WORD was at the top. You were doing God's will if you obeyed the commands found in the Bible. In other words, it would be stupid to pray, "Lord, is it your will for me to become a bank robber?"

(2) BY THE VOICE OF THE WORD meant that God could "illuminate" certain Bible verses as you prayed for God's will. It was kind of like item one, but with some hocus pocus thrown in. Let's say you ask the Lord what to do and then a verse pops into your mind. So you go, "The Lord GAVE ME a verse to guide me." Yeah, we said that a lot. Some members took this too far by "cutting to the Scriptures." Like cutting a deck of cards, you open your Bible at a random spot, stick in your finger and see what verse you pointed to. It was like turning your Bible into a OUIJA board. I tried it a couple of times and realized it was an iffy proposition.

(3) BY DIRECT REVELATION meant that God could give you a personal revelation. Like when I decided to become a teacher. There was no verse in the Bible that said, "Salem, you should be a teacher." But I believed that God had guided me.

(4) BY GODLY COUNSEL was when you got advice from your leaders.

(5) BY CIRCUMSTANCES AND CONDITIONS was an interesting one.

We believed God could cause things to happen—certain *circumstances*—that would help you make a decision. Let's say you planned to go to town and your car broke down. God might be telling you to stay home. (We did not believe in coincidences.) You also had to consider your *conditions*. If you only have one leg you didn't need to pray about a dancing career.

(6) BY BURDENS meant that God could give you a very strong desire to do something. We would say, "I have a burden to take a faith trip. *God laid it on my heart.*"

(7) PUTTING OUT A FLEECE was a term we got from the Old Testament story about Gideon. God told him to do something hard and Gideon put a sheep's woolen fleece on the ground. He asked God to confirm His will by making the fleece wet in the morning while the ground around it stayed dry. So you would pray, "Lord, if you want me to do X, then please cause Y to happen." The fleece method was last on the list because it was supposed to be used sparingly. You wanted to avoid "putting God to the test."

But I thought laying out a fleece sounded like a great idea.

Journal Entry (October 29, 1973) If God wants me to marry Miriam, I asked Him to confirm it by having her love me back. That's my fleece.

November 1973 to February 1976

The little girl said, "I don't like what I see"
"This whole situation is frightening me"
The hungry wolf gave a wink and fiercely smiled
"Some day soon, my dear, I'll have to eat you, child"

THE HONEYMOON IS OVER

THOUGHT ALL THE PREMARITAL boxes had been checked off. The signs indicated a green light for the mission. First there was that big coincidence of meeting Miriam unexpectedly in the Paris colony. (Circumstances and Conditions) In prayer I received a message that God would be pleased with our union. (Direct Revelation) Deborah and Jethro thought it was a good match. (Godly Counsel) I had a strong desire to be with Miriam. (A Burden) Now I just needed for Miriam to feel the same about me. (My Fleece)

I didn't tell Miriam about the fleece. We continued to discuss marriage, but I was careful not to pressure her. I wanted it to be her choice. As the days passed, Miriam seemed more open to the idea. I thought things were moving in the right direction when suddenly there was a setback.

Journal Entry (November 15, 1973) Rachel talked to Miriam and discouraged her from marrying me. Rachel said she didn't think our astrological signs went together well. She also said that since Miriam was older than me, we would have sexual problems.

Astrology? Yep! As if things weren't weird enough, Mo threw astrology into the mix. Personally, I was no stranger to astrology having been introduced to that mumbo jumbo by my Aunt (who was not as tightly wound as my mom). My dear Auntie had jewelry to display her sun sign, consulted her horoscope regularly, visited psychics for readings, and had

Buddha statues around her house. She also had a variety of psychic books hidden on the top shelf of her closet (along with a marital sex manual that was VERY interesting reading for a certain 14 year old boy).

So, we weren't compatible because Miriam was an Aquarius and I was a Leo? Well, thank you, Rachel. Now Miriam was wavering.

"Salem, what if I marry you and then we fall in love with someone else?"

That was a real confidence booster. Why didn't I give up at this point? Hell if I know. But I thought, *"Maybe Rachel is testing us to see if our relationship is genuine. If doubts brake us up, then we should be broken up."*

Then Jethro came to the rescue.

Journal Entry (November 18, 1973) Jethro talked to me about how things were going between Miriam and me. I told him Miriam was having doubts. Jethro said, "I'll talk to her."

I'm not sure what Jethro said to Miriam, but a week later Miriam gave me her final answer.

"I do love you and I think we should get married."

My fleece! ! MY FLEECE! Now all the stars were aligned. Things heated up quickly after that. Miriam and I would sneak off to the bathroom and make out. Hard to believe, but, apart from hugs, this was our first physical contact. One Saturday we went out witnessing together. We rode the trains and hit various cities to sell literature. At the end of the day we found a hotel room for the night. There we were alone in our underwear and guess what happened? Nothing. Just some kissing. Miriam sure looked inviting, but I wasn't about to mess with premarital sex.

At the end of December all the Italian colonies met at Emmanuel's villa in Certaldo for our BETROTHAL (a celebration and official pronouncement that we were a couple). Miriam and I took turns telling how we met and how the Lord guided us to get together. Then Rachel and Emmanuel gave a little talk. When the union was blessed, Miriam and I shared a big kiss in front of the group and the party began—good food and wine, singing and dancing. When the festivities ended, Miriam and I headed into Florence to begin our honeymoon.

After a betrothal it was up to the couple to get legally married—something the Family encouraged. We had no idea how to get legally married in Italy; but then, in a flash, I remembered that INFORMATION BOOTH at the Florence train station. I was delighted to find that very same lady still worked there. When we told her our story, I thought she would explode with excitement.

"Che bello, the young lovers get married in Firenze."

We had come to the right place. This lady went to work and soon we had a list of offices to visit. Off we went to an office and filled out papers, paid a fee, and got a basic document. But that was just the start. There were other offices where we filled out more papers, paid more fees, and got little stamps to put on our marriage certificate. With the paperwork complete, the Mayor of Florence performed the marriage on December 29, 1973.

Sounds romantic, right? But the very next morning Miriam was crying in bed and telling me she thought the whole thing was a big mistake. Great. We didn't even make it a week. The only thing I could think of was to read her verses from the Bible. That went on for about an hour—an emergency therapy session—and finally she calmed down. For the next few days we visited a couple of lovely towns—Lucca and Via Reggio—but it was not a lovely time.

We ran across some Family members who were out witnessing and Miriam said, "They are looking for a place to stay for the night. We should share our room with them."

"No! I don't think that's a good idea. We—just—got—married."

"Salem, that's not a very loving attitude. You should be more revolutionary."

My newlywed wife was giving me grief for not sharing our hotel room. After a week we returned to Certaldo with a dark cloud over our heads. *"So we got off to a rocky start,"* I thought. *"But things have to get better now."* I was wrong. There were just more rocks.

Miriam made it plain she had buyer's remorse. In the following months she made my head spin—I never knew what to expect. She was occasionally sweet, but more often cold and critical. Now she was stuck with me. I kept trying different things to win her over, but got little response. I couldn't figure out what I had done wrong. Why was she acting like this? This left me with a gloomy thought: *The thing that I feared most has come upon me.*

Are you feeling sorry poor little Salem? Taking my side? Good!

All the better to eat you with, my dear.

If I had a time machine I would send this letter back to Miriam in 1974:

Dear Miriam (of the past),

You think you married the wrong person. Guess what? Everyone marries the wrong person. We marry a fantasy and have to live with the reality. You are clueless and don't know what you are doing. Once you get over the shock of me, your heart will soften. Sadly, by then, bitterness will be growing in me like a cancerous lump. The surgery to remove it will be quite painful—for both of us.

Salem (of the future)

When Miriam pissed me off, I would go silent. And Miriam would be like, "Well, just be that way! I don't care." We could go for days without speaking to one another. Then one of us would remember that Christians are supposed to love their enemies and we would trudge on. Part of me wanted to call it quits, but what about all my calculations about finding God's will? So I waited for things to work out according to THE PLAN.

However, a bright spot gradually emerged. Contrary to Rachel's predictions, Miriam and I had no difficulties in bed. Our honeymoon was a failed launch due to bad emotional weather, but after that we enjoyed many successful orbits. At first we slept on my same old mattress in elementary classroom. Later on we moved to the bus parked behind the school and shared it with Ezrom and Cedar. Ezrom and Cedar took the back half; we took the front half. We stretched out a curtain to divide our spacious suites. If we wanted to do more than sleep, we had to negotiate our schedules.

Okay, so sex was no problem; but it didn't resolve the burning question in my heart: *Did Miriam really love me?* One time I wanted to have a special night with Miriam, so we agreed on a time to meet in the evening. I planned it all out—a romantic walk, a bottle of wine, I even wrote her a poem. But Miriam never showed up. I waited and waited and no word. Finally, I gave up on the whole thing and got ready for bed. I was fuming in the dark when Miriam came waltzing in.

"Salem, what are you doing in bed? Didn't we have plans?"

"That was supposed to be hours ago, Miriam. Where were you?"

"Oh, I was talking to a new sister. She's really nice. We were sharing our testimonies."

"Okay, fine...so goodnight. I'm going to sleep."

"I see, now you're all mad at me because I was a little late."

"A little late? You weren't just a little late."

"Well, it's not right for you to go to bed angry."

"What do you expect? I was looking forward to seeing you and you never came."

"Okay. But you're upset and I think we need to make love."

"What? No! That's not going to happen!"

"Oh, yes you are."

My heart was beating wildly and I was shaking. But Miriam was persistent and I eventually gave in—big surprise, right? In the morning I was both pissed and puzzled. What had I tumbled into? Where was my confidence about "God's Will" now? It was dawning on me that I just didn't understand what made Miriam tick. She was a go-with-the-flow artist who flitted from one flower to the next with little thought about time. I, on the other hand, was very organized. If someone told me to meet at 4 PM, I would be there 5 minutes early. My take was: *If Miriam cared about me, she would be on time.* And my insecurity colored the way I interpreted events.

Occasionally we had a good patch and I would write in my journal: *It's a miracle. I think things are working out.* But when things went down a week later I would write: *We're not speaking. She's being bitchy again.*

It made the good times seem like a tease, like Lucy yanking the football away from Charlie Brown. I sunk deep and deeper into my role as the wronged party, like Edmond Dantès, in *The Count of Monte*

Cristo, locked away in the Château d'If prison, nursing my grudge, regretting I ever proposed to Miriam.

However, when I do the math, I can see that when we got married WE BARELY KNEW EACH OTHER. There we were, limping along, barely holding together our relationship. It reminds me of those old films documenting the history of flight. You see these people in their poorly designed flying machines, pedaling like crazy and flapping ridiculous bird wings as they head for the edge of a cliff. That was our marriage—the crash was inevitable.

I AVOIDED THE PAIN BY throwing myself into my work.

The more experience I got in the classroom, the better things went. Leaders complemented the job I was doing and gave me more responsibilities. I didn't mind the extra work, but the complements bothered me (as usual).

Journal Entry (February 16, 1974) The praise I'm getting makes me scared. Will I get lifted up? I know God hates that. I have to trust the Lord to keep me humble.

In April I completed my basic course work and took a train to London where I was signed up for a summer lecture series at the Montessori Training Centre. When I got there I was surprised to discover I was the only male student among thirty or so women. The instructors were two crusty old ladies who were originally trained by Maria Montessori. After weeks of presentations and guided practice sessions we had to pass two examinations. The first, a written one, was no big deal because I studied hard. The second was harder—we had to demonstrate the use of Montessori materials in front of our teachers. I had serious stage fright, but passed. I now possessed a Montessori Teacher's Certificate for the Primary level (3- to 6-year-olds).

While in England I stayed at the Family's Montessori school. Everyone there was full of questions about what it was like to work around Queen Deborah. As head of the childcare ministry worldwide, people would write Deborah and she would send them advice. I was given a tour of the London childcare facility and favored the teachers with some of my best war stories.

Back then squatting was somewhat legal in Britain. The London Family took over an abandoned building and turned it into a disco. They put together a good rock band and passed out flyers to stimulate interest. Some of the sisters even dressed up as go-go girls. There was a drama troupe to perform skits like I had done during my previous time in England. For sure, I was a bit nostalgic as I watched their shows.

The head of the drama troupe was this British guy named Simon Peter. I shared some of my past dramatic adventures with him and he let me brainstorm with the group as they created new material. Their show was wilder than anything I ever put together, with mad scientists, topless girls and poison pie fights. ("I'm too young to pie!")

When I returned to Italy I went back to my duties with the children. Whenever one of the kids had a birthday, I performed a little magic show. I invented a character called "Captain Whammo" with a colorful pair of tights, a flashy American flag T-shirt, goggles, cape and a fright wig. Captain Whammo would run in, do some tricks for the birthday boy or girl, and run out. Later I would come in without the costume and joke with the kids.

"What did I miss?"

The kids yelled, "Captain Whammo was here!"

"Captain Whammo? I wish I had been here."

"Are you Captain Whammo?"

"Me? Of course not. I'm Salem."

Jethro decided to duplicate the London disco scene in the spacious Babe's Ranch building. Soon we had an Italian disco on Saturday nights with crowds of Italian guys coming in every weekend to hear the band and dance with our girls. When Jethro saw me do a magic show for one of his children, he asked me to give a repeat performance on disco night.

The Italians loved it. And then Jethro drafted me to be the drama coordinator for the disco. (Be careful what you wish for, Salem.) Now I was with the kids during the week, "litnessing" on the weekends, and preparing skits for our disco nights.

The whole disco idea was like a jazzed up version of the old "Holy Ghost Sample." We preached about Jesus, but also clearly communicated that the Family was different—not like those stinking churches. With this in mind, I usually came up with two kinds of skits. First we did funny skits that were pretty wild and crazy. I had a great one where we would dress up as acrobats and do silly stunts. We would clap and yell, "HUP, HUP, HEY!" while enthusiastically doing horrible handstands and pitiful cartwheels. That bit was always a hit.

Later we would present a serious skit with a message (like THE FREEZING MAN). When the show was over, someone would speak to the whole crowd and give them the salvation message. Then the Family members at the disco would spread out amongst the crowd to talk to people individually.

On disco nights our girls were supposed to dance with the Italian visitors. If any Italian girls attended, I would occasionally invite them to dance. I was not the best dancer; but Miriam was electric on the dance floor. She tried to give me some pointers, but that made me even more inhibited. One night I was dressed up in my Captain Whammo gear waiting to do my act. There were some go-go girls up on stage dancing to the music and I decided to join in just to get a laugh.

Afterwards Miriam goes, "You were dancing on the stage!"

"Miriam, I hope you're not going to make fun of my dancing."

"No, Salem. You don't get it. Captain Whammo can dance! He must release your inner disco dancer."

"Wow! What do you know? Captain Whammo can dance."

"You are my Captain Whammo."

"I AM your Captain Whammo!"

NO ONE WAS REALLY PREPARED for Mo's next revelation.

Things had pretty much calmed down after SHINERS OR SHAMERS and OLD BOTTLES. But then Mo started writing about something called FLIRTY FISHING. It seems that Mo and Maria experimented with sex appeal as a way to witness to men. In the Flirty Fishing letters, Mo described their experiences in great detail. The climax came when Maria actually had a sexual affair with a young man in order *to show him the love of Jesus.* Mo called it "the ultimate sacrifice" in order to win a soul.

It sounded wild, but I just thought, *"Maybe that's okay for God's prophet."* After all, in the Old Testament you could read stories about God telling His prophets to do pretty crazy stuff—like eating dung, walking around naked, and even marrying prostitutes. So that's the category I put Flirty Fishing in. But so far, the practice hadn't filtered down to us. No one said, "Hey, let's try that Flirty Fishing stuff." It might have been a theoretical possibility, but it wasn't a reality for the average Family member.

I know you're probably thinking, *"Hold on, let me get this straight. First Mo gets you to memorize about a thousand verses and then tosses out the Bible? Claim's he's God's prophet and gets you to sell his whacky letters? And now he's teaching you that sex is a witnessing tool? What kind of shit-for-brains idiots would follow this crackpot?"*

I know. I know. Sounds stupid. But young folks make dumb choices. The light doesn't instantly snap on when you are going the wrong way. Sure I can see things clearly now; but back then I was a true believer. Mo's main tactic—his best trick—was to use *the end of the world strategy:*

"Don't you see? Things were a certain way in the Jewish age. And then Jesus came and ushered in a new age. Now we're in the end-time. It's time for God to change all the rules!"

Believe it or not, I did ponder things. If Mo had said something like *"I just got a revelation that I AM JESUS,"* it would have been quits for me. But what Mo did was to take our core beliefs and twist them slowly, a little here and a little there. When I joined the Family it's like we were all together in this wonderfully warm hot tub. The temperature drop was so gradual we barely felt it going from warm to lukewarm, lukewarm to cold, cold to freezing to death.

DEBORAH BECAME SWAMPED WITH HER childcare ministry.

As the number of letters stacked up, she enlisted Sarah Ireland to help answer all the queries (When should I stop breastfeeding? How soon should I start potty training?) The two of them would consult all kinds of childcare and baby books, trying to find the best response for each needy mother. With Sarah out of the picture, things started to shift around at the school. I was left in charge of the teaching duties and a sister named Lystra stepped in to become the colony leader.

Journal Entry (June 15, 1974) Lystra is now the shepherdess, but I am like her right hand. Since she's not a teacher, she takes most

of my suggestions. She also made me a tribe leader.

I told you about tribes, right? The practice of dividing the Family into tribes may have been a thing of the past, but the term TRIBE LEADER still referred to an older brother or sister in leadership training. I can't remember getting much training; but now I had to read the little reports brothers and sisters filled out each week. I'm sure everyone considered me to be laid back because I never gave anyone flak about what they wrote. Guess what? Those things were boring. It was busy-work bullshit, but I had to start somewhere.

In June a familiar face showed up to help out at the school—Jair, the zealous babe I taught in Kentucky, now all fired up about becoming a teacher. I was happy to have another male to join me in the female dominated childcare ministry. And someone else arrived to work at the school—Miriam. This surprised me because she once told me she never wanted to work with children. But alas, the print shop had been moved to another city. I was thinking, *"Miriam and I will be around each other all day. What am I in for now?"*

It had become clear to me that Deborah and Jethro weren't a couple anymore. They could both be seen with new partners. Then suddenly Jethro (and his new "wife") moved to Paris to head up that area while Deborah (with her new "consort") stayed in Italy. This greatly impacted me because when Jethro wanted to see his children, I would escort them by train to Paris. Meanwhile, when Deborah was busy I would still take care of the kids in Italy. It takes a village (and that village was named Salem).

For the next year I worked in the classroom while training various teaching assistants. At the same time I enrolled in another Montessori course for the elementary level. That meant many late nights hitting the books. Just to make my life interesting, more responsibility came my way in the running of the school. So now I was a minor leader, classroom teacher, drama director, and nanny/baby sitter for Deborah and Jethro's kids.

Of course, I was still expected to go out selling Mo Letter (litnessing). I can sum up my litnessing experience with three words: It Totally Sucked! I really had a crisis of faith about it. Who wants to walk around selling pamphlets for hours at a time? Meanwhile, the Family had some competition—the Moonies exchanged flowers for donations and the Hare Krishnas sold books in airports. As a result, people on the street started steering away from anyone shoving papers at them. When selling Mo Letters got harder, we looked around for new virgin territory. I am pretty sure the Children of God invented the practice of collecting donations at traffic lights.

When I joined the Family I didn't even know there was a leader named Mo. After I was indoctrinated, I grew to appreciate the Mo Letters. But it didn't make sense to distribute them cold to outsiders. We'd sell them and later see the ground littered with them. So what was the point? Just to get money?

In all the literature, Mo was illustrated as a lion. Some of Mo's letters were inspirational; but others I'd put in the "acquired taste" category. Like when Mo announced he had a spirit helper named Abrahim, a gypsy who died long ago and was now assigned to give psychic guidance to the Family. See what I mean? And then there were Mo's countless dreams (many of them sexual), published in great detail complete with illustrations. What was one to do with all the weirdness?

Everybody else seemed to think this was heavy stuff; so I tried hard to wring out some significance. I went with the crowd and never dared to mutter, *"The Emperor has no clothes."* But when Mo's prophecies started to fail, it was harder to handle.

Journal Entry (January 11, 1975) I'm having some trials about some of the things Mo has written. Nixon didn't become a dictator like Mo predicted and America hasn't fallen yet. Maybe Mo interpreted things wrong. I think it's important to remember that even though Mo is anointed, he is just a man. He can make mistakes.

In time, I rationalized Mo's predictive errors. We all wanted Mo to be a perfect prophet, but he wasn't. I still thought of him as a father who loved us—and fathers aren't right about everything. But the big thing that kept me clinging onto Mo was my belief that God led me to the Family. If God didn't want me following Mo, wouldn't he tell me to stop? Why would God have allowed me to go on a false path? Meanwhile, I had my own prophetic dream.

Journal Entry (April 5, 1975) I dreamed Miriam had a baby.

After over a year of marriage, Miriam and I had reached a détente of sorts. I knew our marriage needed work and was ready for a miracle.

Journal Entry (April 23, 1975) Miriam is now pregnant. Praise God!

Not long after this discovery, Deborah had a meeting to announce her own big news. The school was relocating to Massa, a town near the west coast of Italy. Furthermore, SHE DECIDED TO PUT ME IN CHARGE. Me? An actual colony shepherd? There's a big difference between being in charge of children and being in charge of grown-ups. I didn't know what trouble was until I was made a leader.

An Italian named Giovanni owned the Massa house and rented it to us for a small amount. He was probably surprised to get any money out of the place because it was falling apart. But the Family had plenty of able-bodied workers to make it livable. The main floor had a spacious kitchen connected to huge dining area. We put shelves for the Montessori equipment against one wall and the kids worked at the dining tables. The upper floor had bedrooms and two bathrooms. There was also an attic space just large enough for all the children's bunk beds.

At the end of that summer I returned to London for the Montessori elementary training program. While in England, the leaders asked me if I would share some of my experience with all of their mothers, teachers and miscellaneous childcare workers. Sounded good to me. That night I found myself facing a huge room full of sisters who looked at me like I was an educational rock star. I told them the story of how I was called to be a teacher, gave them some charming anecdotes, and sang as many children's songs as I could remember. The big finish was a Q and A time. That's when a couple of things came to me. First, these ladies—mostly new moms—were starving for information about how to raise their kids. Second, I didn't know what the hell I was talking about. I had only been teaching for a few years and these guys thought I had all the answers.

Back in Italy my head was spinning with ideas. It was clear to me that Deborah's method for helping parents—all that letter writing—wasn't doing the job. Why couldn't we write some kind of handbook? Meanwhile, Deborah moved to a little Italian municipality called Zoagli not too far from Massa. When I took the children to see her, I mentioned my instruction booklet idea; but it didn't seem to appeal to her.

Journal Entry (September 23, 1975) Rachel and Emmanuel headed up a regional conference for all the Italian colonies. Mother Eve was there and asked to see me. She said she could see my positive influence on the children's lives and that I was anointed by God to be a teacher.

You see what I had to deal with? *"Mother Eve says you're anointed."* But I shouldn't have worried about getting too full of myself because there was a humbling gadfly coming my way. And his name was Paul Bunyan. He arrived in Italy one day; he was tall with shaggy blond hair and a beard. All he needed was a horned Viking helmet to complete the picture. He wore wooden clogs so you could hear him clickety-clacking all over the place. He had this huge wooden box he personally constructed to carry his guitar—it actually looked more like a child's coffin. Paul stored all kinds of things in there—like *Felix the Cat* with his magic bag. I thought he was just passing through, but Paul latched himself onto the school, helping out with chores and playing with the kids.

Paul Bunyan was a real showboat. (HA HA HA HA... that's me laughing at myself because my Texas tormentors said the same thing about me.) Anyway, it wasn't long before Paul had the single sisters swooning. The children loved him, of course, and crawled all over him like little lap dogs. I was the colony leader, but Paul kept sending me who-do-you-think-you-are vibes. This irked me, of course, and I hoped this guy would move on soon. No such luck.

"Paul Bunyan, my dear rival and chief challenger, you did me a great service because you were always available to push a pin in my balloon. I may have been the Massa leader, but you were always ready with some

sly condescension."

Apart from Paul's know-it-all attitude clashing with my know-it-all attitude, Massa was a pleasant place to live, right next to a forest with hidden fig trees just waiting to be plundered. A beautiful beach was just a short drive away. Our landlord, who lived in a hilltop home with his wife and mother, took a liking to me and would invite me for dinner and conversation. Giovanni did speak a bit of English, but my Italian was getting to the point where I could converse easily. Along with the other teachers and assistants, we had several Italian disciples living there. They also helped boost my language skills.

When Jethro sent a request for me to bring his children to Paris for a visit, he arranged for me to stay at the Paris childcare center. Again, around all the teachers and parents, it was like a repeat performance of my London experience—CHILDCARE MESSIAH! Okay, I admit, it was fun. I was like—like Chance the gardener in Being There, mistaken for a big shot. But I should have been paying attention because I had just entered a danger zone. It started off innocently enough when Jethro invited me to go on a picnic with the kids.

After the meal, Jethro said, "Salem, you shouldn't be stuck in one little school. If you and Miriam move to Paris, I'll put you in charge of our whole childcare operation."

"Wow. I don't know what to say. What would Deborah think about it?"

"Deborah! She's just holding you back. In Paris you can help us set up several schools and travel around training the teachers."

"I will talk to Miriam and we'll give it some serious thought and prayer."

This was an alluring proposition. I was excited by the prospect, but also nervous. Would I be able to handle such responsibilities? In a few days I was back in Italy and discussed it with Miriam. We soon came to a decision and I wrote a letter to Jethro accepting his offer. But a storm was headed my way.

When Deborah got wind of Jethro's plot, she immediately ratted him out to her father, Mo. Then she hauled ass to the school in Massa. She was pissed, but mostly at Jethro. As for me, she used the fear tactic.

"Salem, you're not mature enough for such a big ministry. If you insist on going, I don't think God will bless it. I think you'll have some big problems."

"But I do think there is a need for teacher training."

"If you stay in Italy, I'll let you write some childcare booklets for publication."

That was the carrot. (Hey, wasn't that my idea to begin with?) So, it was a short war and Deborah won—Miriam and I caved under the pressure. Jethro told me later that Mo sent him a nasty note about "stealing Deborah's childcare worker." I was sorry about that; but I had worked with Deborah's children for over three years and owed her quite a bit. Way back in England she was the one who encouraged me to get into teaching—something I wouldn't have done without her encouragement.

Journal Entry (October 6, 1975)   God told me Miriam will have a baby boy. She is much more loving to me now. I had a revelation that I wasn't yielding to the marriage because I was subconsciously punishing Miriam for the past.

"Salem, this baby growing inside of me is just like our love growing for each other."

"Miriam, I hope that's true. We need to get our act together and work as a team."

So we started talking more and I thought God was giving us another chance. Maybe our marriage story would have a happy ending. Maybe we would become powerful leadership partners as we pioneered the childcare field for the Family all over the world.

Then something strange happened. In November I got a message from Rachel requesting that I meet her in Rome. While Jethro ruled over France and northern Europe, Rachel and Emmanuel were the top leaders in Italy and southern Europe. So this was a big deal. I couldn't imagine why I was summoned.

When we were alone, Rachel asked, "Are you happy working with Deborah?"

"Uh...happy? Well, I love her children and Massa is a nice place to live."

She squinted her eyes. "That's not an answer. I heard about what happened when Jethro invited you to Paris. How did you feel about it?"

"It was a tough decision, but I think Deborah was right. I'm not ready for such a leadership position."

"Hmm. I agree with Jethro—Deborah does hold onto you too tightly. And you know, she's not right about everything."

"Getting Jethro in trouble was the worst thing that happened."

"Salem, you should know some changes are coming. Soon you will have a big decision to make. I just wanted you to be ready."

I returned to Massa and told Miriam about this mysterious conversation. We didn't quite know what to make of it. There were some crucial puzzle pieces missing.

Meanwhile, Miriam was getting huge. As the delivery approached, we went to a nearby hospital to arrange things. After an examination, the doctor gave us the news that our baby was in the breach position. He tried to talk us into a C-section. As we walked down the hallway, he described the operation.

"So simple, just a little cut here and..."

That's the last thing I remember. I passed out and woke up several minutes later laid out on an examination table. There was Miriam, crying, and the doctor, looking like he had seen it all.

Back at home, Deborah—who popped out babies like candy bars from a vending machine—assured us a C-section wasn't necessary. So we went ahead with the natural birth option. A few weeks later, when the time came, we zipped to a local hospital. Miriam was whisked away by nurses and I was assigned to the waiting room. I wasn't freaking out until I heard Miriam screaming. Then I got nervous. But after a long wait, an excited nurse burst into the room carrying a baby all bundled up.

"*Un Bambino,*" she said, "*Molto grasso.*" (A boy...very fat.)

Miriam was happy, but wiped out, and spent the night at the hospital. The next day we returned to Massa. Everyone reacted as you typically do when someone has a baby. It was a blessed time.

Journal Entry (December 30, 1975) On Tuesday night at 7:40 God gave us a son. We decided to call him Robin.

One day we got a surprise visitor—a sister named Esther who was married to one of Mo's sons, Hosea. She was well known in the Family for her beautiful voice. That night she graced us with several songs before returning to Certaldo where she was living at the time. That was all well and good, but I was surprised when Esther's guest appearances became a regular thing—she just kept popping by. I noticed Paul Bunyan was paying an awful lot of attention to her. In fact, they seemed quite cozy together. Then Esther asked Paul to accompany her to Certaldo—seems she needed some help with a project.

As time went by, we saw less and less of Paul. I wondered, *"How much help does this lady need?"* When Deborah got wind of this, she asked me to track Paul down and get him back to the school. Still clueless about what was going on, I managed to get Paul on the phone and fussed at him a bit about shirking his duties at the school.

Not long after this we got another surprise visit from Esther's husband, Hosea. He sat me down and began a cross-examination about Paul's relationship with Esther.

"Brother Salem, how many times has Esther been here to visit?"

"I haven't kept count, but lots."

"When Paul leaves, how long is he gone?"

"Sometimes he stays gone for days."

"Did you give him permission to go?"

"Uh, not really. It's just that Esther asked for his help."

"Didn't you think it might have been a good idea to let me know what was going on?"

"What is going on?"

The thing is, I really DIDN'T know what was going on. For all I knew Paul was helping Esther move furniture. It's true that Miriam walked in on them once and saw Esther sitting on Paul's lap. But I never suspected hanky-panky. That was pretty much the end of the interview. But in a few days a rather subdued Paul returned to the school and stayed put. We never discussed Hosea's visit.

In February the Paul and Esther issue was abruptly eclipsed. The big mystery Rachel hinted at was unveiled. Mo issued an executive command—Deborah and Jethro were ordered to Lima, Peru in order to take over the Family's missionary thrust into South America. Rachel was right; I did have a big decision to make. I could stay in Europe or I could go to South America. Deborah assured me that if I stayed with her she would give me time to write childcare instruction booklets for the Family. So, I chose South America.

And wouldn't you know it, Paul Bunyan was coming along as well. Did Hosea have something to do with that? I wonder.

9

March 1976 to December 1978

The Hatter spreads a table with tea and riddles
There's crazy on both sides and madness in the middle
At his little party nothing's quite what it seems
And everything is wilder than your wildest dreams

184

IT ALL GOES SOUTH

WE TOOK A BREAK TO let our parents meet their grandson.

That's basically how we got passage to South America—my folks paid for our flight from Italy and Miriam's folks paid for the flight to Peru. Of course, everyone was delighted to meet the baby—grandchildren are always exciting. After a few weeks, we left my father's house loaded with baby gear. Next stop was Alabama to meet Miriam's folks. It would be my first encounter with her roots.

Miriam's father was raised in poverty, just like my dad. He was ashamed of his upbringing and dropped out of high school to join the Navy. After his service in the military, he earnestly desired to establish himself in a higher, more respectable class. He worked hard to maintain a new image and become obsessively concerned about appearances. This affected Miriam because her father tended to be highly critical of her hairstyles, clothing, and her choice of friends. Due to this constant scrutiny, Miriam's father passed down his feelings of inferiority.

Miriam's mother—the one who gave her daughter the acceptance and emotional security she craved—died in childbirth when Miriam was 13 years old. That left quite a void. A few years later, her dad married again—this time to a long-legged blond trophy wife.

During our visit, Miriam's father—who always dressed like he was ready to play golf—was pretty well behaved. He was a charming salesman full of many funny stories. That was good because I had none for him. (I learned quickly that our parents didn't care to hear about our gypsy life.) Despite his buddy-buddy projection, I could tell it was an

185

effort for Miriam's father to relate to me. I was out of his realm of experience.

Miriam's stepmother, who habitually carried either a cigarette or diet cola in her hand, likewise seemed full of southern hospitality. But I sensed a certain I'm-sizing-you-up attitude. Sure enough, after a few days of restraint, she cornered me in the kitchen one morning.

"Just how long do you plan to keep this up?"

Puzzled, I replied, "Keep what up?"

"Bumming around the world, living off your daddy's money."

"I don't know what you're talking about. I don't live off my daddy's money."

"You must live on something."

"The Lord supplies all our needs."

"Well isn't that nice for you? The rest of us have to work for a living."

I already knew Miriam charted high on the emotional-sensitivity scale; but now, around her father and stepmother, I saw parts of her personality that filled in some blanks. I sensed she had an interrupted life and still grieved over the loss of her mother. She was discontented about many things—past and present. But I didn't know what to do about it. I felt like a big failure as a husband.

As page after page of my journal testifies, fretting over past failures was one of my preoccupations. So I hoped things would go better in South America. Maybe my third continent would be the charm. (Having a fresh start was a motif for me: Things are going to be different now.)

Miriam and I arrived in Lima, Peru on March 7, 1976 and began phase two of our service under Deborah and Jethro. We were temporarily placed in a house with several other disciples while Deborah scouted out a location for the new school. Meanwhile, Jethro was hot to get some kind of disco action going. He used our house because it had a fairly large living room where we could invite Peruvians to party. We had no band, so we played tape cassettes through large speakers. Predictably, Jethro asked me to organize some drama to liven up the place.

I enlisted some South American Family members to round out the cast. Jordán, a local Peruvian brother, was my first contact. He spoke pretty good English and took me to meet Simón, a brother from

Argentina. We went to a bar and hashed out our plans over bottles of beer (cerveza was one of my first Spanish words). Soon we had our show sketched out. When we needed a female for a part, we would pull in a sister named Margarita—a flaming hot Peruvian all the single guys lusted after.

Our little troupe was a hit and soon we branched out to local parks and plazas to do our "Holy Ghost Sample" thing. A favorite location was a square in Miraflores. In the beginning most of my parts were silent because I only knew a smattering of Spanish. But Spanish was similar to Italian and easy to pick up.

I found this list of our sketches in my journal:

The Freezing Man	**The Communist Plan**
The Drunk Man	**The Cowboys**
The Hypnotist	**Kung Fu Fighter**
Free Tickets to Heaven	**Randy Skit**
The Dreamer	**The Acrobats**
The Waiter	**The Magician**

Mi buen amigo, Jordan.

Jordán, Simón and I became the three musketeers, planning our shows and generally hanging out. We liked to visit Jordán's lovely parents and give them previews of our funny skits. Then we would watch some Peruvian television—mainly old American programs that were dubbed into Spanish. I'm talking old stuff, like *The Rifleman* and *Gilligan's Island*.

While this was all great fun, I began to wonder what was going on with my childcare ministry. Finally, in April we were told a house for the school had been found in a district outside of Lima called Chaclacayo. Miriam and I moved out there with Robin and were soon joined by Paul Bunyan.

Paul and Nina

All the school materials had arrived in boxes. As the designated leader/shepherd, it was up to me to arrange the classrooms and bedrooms. The house had three levels. The rooms on the lower level were used as a sleeping area for the children and a few school helpers. The middle level had a kitchen, dining room, living room, and a small bedroom for Miriam and me. The top floor had three rooms—two large ones we used as classrooms and one small one for Paul Bunyan and his new wife, Bethany. We were on a lovely piece of property with poinsettia, banana, and avocado trees. A small Peruvian man tended the garden—I think he came with the house—and would hang bunches of bananas outside our kitchen door.

It wasn't long before the school opened for business. I had all my usual duties: teaching, organizing schedules, and working with our little drama crew. Whenever I had time, I drafted a variety of childcare handbooks. After a few months things seemed to be going very well: (1) the children were happy in school, (2) I had completed about three compositions on various educational subjects, (3) Miriam and I were doing better, (4) our son, Robin, was progressing delightfully through all the baby book stages of development, and (5) Paul Bunyan and I had established a shaky peace treaty and only occasionally bumped heads. Life seemed good.

One September night at the school, I was awakened by the noise of our whole house vibrating through a small earthquake. When it ended, all the dogs in the neighborhood started barking. It was pretty scary. But it was nothing compared to the tumultuous shaking that was in store for me.

The Chaclacayo kids with Bethany, Paul and me in the back row.

A few days later something strange happened to Robin.

He was in his highchair and started gulping and staring into space. After a minute or so he slumped over drowsily. We didn't know what to think of it and hoped it would pass—but it didn't. And as the weeks went by, it became clear our son was having convulsions.

Our first reaction was to call for prayer. Deborah and Jethro came over and even brought Mo's daughter, Faithy. With all these heavy hitters gathered, we expected a healing. But the convulsions continued. This launched me into a heart-searching spiral. I needed answers. Was my faith weak? Had I committed some sin that blocked the healing? Was God testing me? I had claimed all the right Scriptures and confessed all the sins I could think of; nevertheless, each day Robin's condition became more severe.

By November we could tell that Robin was getting weaker. And then one horrible night his convulsions increased in number and intensity like

189

nothing I had seen before. Robin would turn red in the face, grimace and then start to spasm violently with his left fist clinched and waving. There would be a brief period of calm when I would try to comfort him, but then another fit would begin. As I held him, each seizure would rack both our bodies. Robin was having continuous seizures. It was hard for me to breath because I was so overcome by panic. My child was dying in my arms.

We rushed Robin to a hospital where he was given an anticonvulsant injection. The doctor recommended that we go to the medical center in Lima for a complete exam and diagnosis. It just so happened that Margarita's mother was a top doctor at Lima's main hospital—the best facility in Peru. By the time the appointment was scheduled, Robin—who previously walked on his own—was no longer able to even stand up. He was examined and given a variety of tests with the equipment available; but the doctors could find no cause for his seizures. We were told Robin probably had epilepsy and that anticonvulsant medication was our only option.

The little pills did help, but made Robin groggy. Of course, Miriam and I felt guilty about giving them to Robin. The Family taught that God was willing and able to heal all sickness—as long as you had faith. Here I was, supposedly a leader, but my prayers for healing were not answered. And now my child was suffering because of my second-rate faith. It had to be my fault. Somehow.

Robin would go for periods with no problems and we would rejoice. Then the seizures would reappear. Miriam and I kept trying to be good disciples, hoping that we would be rewarded with a miraculous healing. As could be expected, various leaders would approach us with questions about Robin's affliction. There was always a subtle undertone of judgment: *There has to be a reason. What is God trying to teach you? Are you seeking the Lord?* None of this counsel was helpful. Where could I find the answer?

Then I remembered the guy in the Bible named Job. He's the one who endured all sorts of sickness and tragedy. I had read it before, but can't say I got much out of it. So I read it again and was quite stunned. Chapter after chapter described Job's struggle to come to terms with his afflictions. The best part was when Job's "friends" come to comfort him. One after another they pronounced similar judgments: *These bad things have happened to you because God is punishing you. Repent of your sins and God will help you.* Hey! This sounded familiar. At the end of the book I was delighted to read that God was angry with Job's friends for their harsh presumptions.

This was like a ray of light. Job was not being punished for some great sin. God had a totally different agenda. Job kept asking God why he had to suffer, but never got a clear answer. Nevertheless, Job continued to trust God. That actually sounded good to me. When it came to Robin's affliction, I could deal with a mystery better than trying to come up with reasons. So with this little encouragement tucked away in my heart, I kept plugging along.

I continued my teaching duties at the school while writing childcare instruction materials on the side. After reviewing my rough drafts, Deborah had a secretary type them up. My booklets were designed to help families use the Montessori Method with their children. How do you teach the basic subjects? How do you organize a school day in your home? Deborah even found an artist to illustrate them. With much excitement we sent them off to be approved by the head of Worldwide Publications back in Italy. I looked forward to their distribution, like one of my dreams coming true. I waited for months, but that stamp of approval never came. Nothing ever got printed.

Toward the end of the year, Paul Bunyan had the great idea to have our Peruvian brothers translate Family songs into Spanish. This went on for weeks and after each song was translated, Paul would teach it to the children. When we took the children out to distribute literature, Paul would have them assemble in one of the many town squares in Lima to sing for a crowd. The reaction was fantastic.

Eventually, Paul's little singing group was invited to be on a children's television program called

"Villa Juguete" (Toy Town). Their appearance on the show was a hit and they were invited back. Jethro asked if I could write a few sketches for the children to perform. The first one I whipped out was essentially a children's version of our old "Randy Skit." (Kid goes to school. Has problems. Prays for help. Enter angels singing about Jesus. Standard Salem script.) With a collection of Spanish songs and sketches to perform, the children's group, *Los Niños de Dios*, became regulars on television.

The children's group performing a skit on the television show (above) and (below) singing at a Peruvian orphanage.

I would usually accompany the children when they went out to do a show. One day we were invited to perform at a local music festival. Remember what I said about Peruvian television? Well, I can't explain it, but for some reason Peruvians flipped for *The Munsters*. At the festival, before the children performed, we watched a Peruvian comedy troupe dressed up as the Munsters. They were hilarious. I wondered how our kids could top that. But when our children started singing, they stole the show.

Here's a picture of four of our girls posing with the Peruvian Munsters.

Remember Ezrom, my good buddy from both TSC and Italy? Well, he and his wife, Cedar, had also moved with us to Peru. Cedar was Deborah's secretary and Ezrom did what he always did—handy man stuff. But one night I was invited over to Deborah and Jethro's house for Ezrom and Cedar's going-away party. They had been invited to be a part of Mo's household. I had no idea where they were going—Mo's location was top secret—but I celebrated Ezrom's good fortune. *Wow! Living with the prophet… what a thrill that will be.* I didn't realize how essential Ezrom's departure would be for my future. The dominos were being set up.

MEANWHILE, MO KEPT ON WRITING about sexual freedom.

All I knew was that no free sex was happening in my little school world. I guessed it was just for some super-spiritual leaders. But as more Mo letters were published, the message became clear:

> *God's only law is love. Sex is God's gift to men and women. The devil has corrupted this gift for his evil purposes. Now it is time for us to take back the freedoms for God's glory. It should be like the Garden of Eden. In the Family we can behave like everyone is married to everyone. For those outside the Family, sex can be used to show God's love for the lost.*

Mo put together a variety of Bible verses that seemed to support this new doctrine. On top of that, we now had our prophet's seal of approval. Our minds whirled. *If we have sex with someone we're not married to, as long as our motivation is to love them, then it's not wrong.* It took quite a while for Mo to work us up to it, but sexual freedom and sexual witnessing gradually became our new commission.

Pretty hard to make that jive with the Bible, right? But most Family members came from the sexually liberated hippie generation. Besides that, we were young, locked and loaded. So, it didn't take much. What's that? God loves it when you have sex? Cool! Our Pied Piper prophet played his flute for us and led us into his dark secret cave. Previously, I had rejected the notion of sex outside of marriage. Now I laughed at what a babe I was. But even though we had permission, there was no big sexual explosion in my little school world.

Journal Entry (December 19, 1976) I used to think I knew so much. But I really knew next to nothing. Do I know a lot now? Or will I look back years from now and laugh?

It was a tantalizing proposition, but really, I was too busy for free sex. When 1977 arrived, Deborah sent me on a supervisory trip to Ecuador to check out their childcare set-ups and to give them teaching advice. They were doing their best with very little support. I returned and told Deborah that if this was an example of what was going on in South America, parents desperately needed training. As a result we organized a two-week workshop for all the teachers and parents in South America.

I patterned the workshop after the ones I had attended at the Montessori Centre in London—lectures in the morning and practice sessions in the afternoon. On March 3rd, over twenty sisters showed up for the training. I gave most of the lessons while Deborah sat at the back and felt free to chime in with little pearls of wisdom. She would also give me a "nix it" signal if she felt I was rambling. Even with a censor, I was on a high. But the buzz didn't last long

In a few weeks we began receiving educational instructional materials printed at the Worldwide Publications Center in Italy. None of it was my stuff. What the hell? There were little booklets on how to teach your child to read and do math—everything I had already worked on. The crew in Italy also produced a set of readers for the children—the *Mo Lion Readers*. In the stories Mo was depicted as a talking lion, of course, teaching kids about Jesus. I looked over the materials with disappointment. This was supposed to be my job. My instruction manuals had been ready for over a year, but had been replaced.

Okay, so that was my first bitter reaction. But when I took a breath and closely examined the Italian products, I was irked even more. In my opinion they were poorly conceived and pretty useless. *The crown has been jerked out of my hands for this junk?* Deborah was likewise deflated, but soon came up with an alternative plan.

"Salem, we should focus our energies on setting up Montessori schools all over South America. As we train the teachers, we can use our own educational manuals."

"That is very ambitious, Deborah."

"But every Montessori school will be a positive testimony of God's love."

It just so happened that a large house in Lima was offered for our use. To start off our new mission, Deborah wanted me to move there to set up a second school. The hitch was that someone had to take over for me at our Chaclacayo School. Guess who? I was instructed to train Paul. (Me training Paul—was that even possible?) Our first session consisted of us giving each other CONSTRUCTIVE CRITICISM over a bottle of wine.

"Sometimes you come across as an arrogant prick."

"Right back at you, brother."

But it turned out to be a good thing. We did manage to hash out some old personality clashes. After giving Paul the keys to my kingdom, I moved my wife and child into town to a big house on Angamos Street.

Journal Entry (May 28, 1977) Paul Bunyan took over Chaclacayo as the colony leader. I hope he does a good job. I have learned a lot from Paul. We are both pretty stubborn. But now I see him in a different light.

I found myself in charge of a really big house in the city with lots of rooms. Predictably, the house was soon crammed with brothers and sisters and their children. Many of these folks were in transition, soon to be moved to other locations in South America; so you didn't have much time to establish deep relationships. Besides, many of them were former leaders from America, making it even more difficult. They weren't used to being under anyone's supervision, especially not little Salem the schoolteacher. I soon missed the peaceful atmosphere I enjoyed back in Chaclacayo.

To handle the stress I turned to my friend, Jordán. When he heard I had never seen a Kung Fu movie he was shocked and immediately carted me to a badly dubbed Bruce Lee movie. (By the way, you do not need to understand Spanish to follow a Kung Fu movie.) Afterwards it became our guilty pleasure to see all the Kung Fu movies that came to Lima.

ONE DAY A VENEZUELAN GIRL named Luz approached me.

She worked as a helper at the school and was a cute little thing with long curly brown hair. Luz shyly asked to speak with me privately. I thought she was having a trial and needed a spiritual pep talk. Turns out she needed more than that.

"Salem, there is a man I have witnessed to. He is very interested in the Family."

"That's great, Luz. Do you need some tips?"

"I think I should show him God's love. I want to Flirty Fish him."

"Uh…alright, if you are sure about it. That's what the Mo letters say to do."

"I have prayed about it."

"Do you have the faith to do it?"

"Yes, but I have a problem. I am virgin. I don't know how to make love."

"I see. That could be a problem."

"Can you teach me?"

My brain screeched to a halt. Weren't any hunky South American brothers available?

"Me? Why me?"

"Because I see you with children, Salem. You will be nice with me."

"Okay. I'll pray about it."

So I had come to a fork in the road. Before going any further I had to speak with my wife. The fact that Luz had approached me, and not the other way around, helped my case when Miriam and I discussed it. You know, it's kind of hard to interpret body language when you ask your wife for permission to have sex with another woman; so I really can't say what was going through Miriam's head when I presented it to her. She took it all in and finally agreed. But really, what else could she have done? We were supposed to be set free from the old law and now under the new "Law of Love."

With the plan approved, Luz and I arranged for an evening together. The time came and—with wine and candlelight—I gave her my very best "instructions." I was gentle and Luz was sweet. We parted with a hug. Mission accomplished.

If that had been the end of it, things might have turned out differently. But sex changes things between people. Luz and I started to spend more time together and it got complicated. She was a charming girl and I was a young buck. I enrolled Luz in night school and gave her more private tutoring. Uh oh! Miriam had not agreed to these repeat performances. Trouble was headed my way.

Journal Entry (June 28, 1977) Miriam is going through a hard time with my sexual sharing. She is extremely jealous. She told me I am giving Luz the love that I should be giving her. It seems like a mess now. I pray things will work out.

But it didn't work out. Miriam freaked out and wrote a letter to Jethro complaining about what was going on. Jethro got steamed up and drove over from his lair and called for a meeting at the Angamos colony. When everyone gathered, Jethro rebuked me in front of the whole group.

"Your so-called shepherd is not handling things in love. As a result you are all suffering. I look around and you all look like spiritual skeletons. What do you have to say for yourself, Salem?"

"I was just trying to obey the Mo Letters."

"Well, you're out of the spirit and in the flesh. You need to apologize to everyone for being a bad example."

After my verbal chastisement, I went back to my room in a daze. I didn't get it. Sure I was sorry that Miriam was hurt, but the Mo Letters were pretty explicit on the subject of sexual sharing. In my mind, I was just pursuing the new freedom outlined by our prophet. I must admit that the main emotion flowing through my body was rage. Did Jethro think I was blind? Everyone now knew that Jethro—along with all the top leadership—had been up to sexual shenanigans for years. So why was Jethro giving me grief?

Later Deborah had a private meeting with me.

"Salem, I was surprised to hear that you had started sharing with Luz without consulting me first."

"I thought I was helping her out. Like the Mo Letters say."

"Still, I could have warned you—things can get pretty messy."

"You're right about that."

I was in the doghouse for now. So I fastened on a humble face and dove into my work with the teachers and children. This whole sexual revolution thing was downright confusing. I had no way of knowing that in a short while certain events would radically change the landscape.

BY AUGUST, OUT OF THE blue, Jethro was out of the picture.

Jethro, Paul Bunyan and the children just packed up and moved to Columbia. It happened so fast. The cover story was they were going on a singing tour; but I had a sneaking suspicion something was up. Deborah was still in Peru and kept a very low profile. I certainly wasn't hearing a single word about our new enthusiastic plan to plant schools all over the continent. The vibes were heavy in the air.

We continued to give my son, Robin, his anticonvulsant medication; but he still had occasional seizures. At least he was walking again. I kept up my mantra: *If I am dedicated enough, if I work hard enough, if I am humble enough, perhaps God will heal him.* If I could figure it out, or pray the perfect prayer, maybe all my doubts would be blown away.

Journal Entry (September 3, 1977) Things started off okay with Luz, but I can see that I got tripped off. I had lots of silly ideas about her.

I was still the colony shepherd at Angamos. And then two familiar faces moved into the house: Cephas, who enlisted me into the Family, and Amminadab, one of the Family's top musicians. I knew them both from my time at TSC. They arrived with their wives and children and set up shop. Cephas was now shacking up with Mo's daughter, Faithy. Meanwhile, Amminadab had hooked up with Cephas' first wife, Shiloh. (It was hard to keep up with all the marital shuffling.) I was happy when Amminadab organized his own children's singing group and asked me to accompany them to their performances. Amminadab—quite a character—was not shy about using his kids to collect donations. We always returned to the colony flush with cash.

Then in November I got some truly shocking news. My good buddy Ezrom—who went to work at Mo's house—had just been kicked out of the Family. In a letter Mo described his downfall: *Ezrom couldn't handle the sexual freedom and was jealous if his wife was going to bed with another man. He was a devil and had to be cast out for the good of the Family.* What the...? This was especially hard to hear because I dearly loved Ezrom. Was I such a bad judge of character?

In December Deborah came breezing through the colony. Like all of Mo's children, she had these eyes that could burn bright with inspiration. But now the glow was different, like she had drunk too many cups of coffee. She told me that we should abandon all our big children's ministry plans and just focus on loving God and witnessing to lost souls. It was a pretty good act—like a "Stepford Wife." Soon Deborah left Peru altogether and joined Jethro and her children.

In early 1978 a new leader named Shaul arrived in town. He gathered all the local colonies together at Angamos for a summit meeting. Our jaws dropped as he lobbed one bomb after another. The big news was that Mo was doing away with all the former leadership because they had abused their power. In fact, there would no longer be any big leaders— just Mo at the top. Colony leaders were to be elected by the members living in each home.

This was like a revolution within the revolution. All of the former leaders were now demoted to regular member status and expected to witness and distribute literature like everyone else. Mo was ESPECIALLY pissed with the old leadership because they had blocked his passionate new doctrines: sexual freedom amongst Family members and Flirty Fishing to win new converts. As for Deborah and Jethro, they were being exiled to Australia.

Mo was now in charge of everything. There would be no more big leaders—except for Mo, our benevolent king and his faithful queen, Maria. So what was Shaul's position? It seems that Mo had created a new position called "Visiting Servant." Shaul's first task was to travel around and spread the news about all the changes as Mo's South American representative. It's hard to remember all the new lingo we used back then, but I think Shaul's title was *King and Queen's Servant* (KQS for short).

A few days later Shaul asked to speak with me personally. Uh, oh! Since I was closely associated with Deborah, I expected my head to go on the block.

"Am I in trouble, Shaul?"

"Absolutely not! We think you have been doing a good job here with the children."

"So what am I supposed to do now?"

"We want you to move back to Chaclacayo and run the place until Rachel arrives.

"Rachel is coming?

"Yes, she's the one who put in a good word for you. She's coming to visit South America later this year and has a message for you."

A message from Rachel? What could that be? Rachel, the one who called me to Rome and gave me a warning about Deborah, was evidently still looking out for me. But it was surprising she still had any clout. Wasn't she formerly a big cheese? I guessed that some cheeses were more rotten than others.

So we packed up and moved back to Chaclacayo. Shaul said there was a detailed Mo Letter about the new revolution coming out soon. Officially, all the changes were to begin on Mo's birthday—February 18th. Until then we had no clear guidance except for one: sexual sharing between Family members was encouraged. This was loud and clear. And the general consensus was, *"Message Received!"*

As Mo's birthday approached, we decided to commemorate it with a party. We invited all the members from Lima—as many as could make it. We got prepared with wine, beer and food. That evening the Chaclacayo house was filled with brothers and sisters. The drinks flowed freely and soon we were singing and dancing in honor of our loving prophet, Moses David. I'm not exactly sure who went first, but as things progressed the clothes came off and we celebrated in the nude. It seemed beautiful to us, our very own Woodstock (minus the mud). The festivities soon overflowed outside with all of us prancing around the trees in the garden *au naturel*.

Mo's birthday letter was entitled "Happy Rebirthday—The RNR Rules. It laid out the basic plan for the "Reorganization and Naturalization Revolution" (RNR for short). Since all the former leaders were fired, new shepherds were to be elected by the colony members. But shepherds were now called "servants" and colonies were now called "homes." These homes could not be more than 12 members and no more than 50% of the members in a foreign country could be American.

All members, even the leaders, were to spend at least 2 hours a day selling literature. And besides passing out Mo Letters, Flirty Fishing was now established as an excepted witnessing practice. And of course, sexual freedom amongst members was now the norm. After the letter was read, I somehow got a vote of confidence as the "servant" of Chaclacayo. I guess folks remembered the thrashing I endured from Jethro. So I was golden.

Because it was expected, Miriam had to accept the sexual sharing— even if she was kind of bipolar about it. She didn't seem to have a problem with the Mo's new doctrine; but when it involved me and other women, it got dicey. I wasn't going nuts with the freedom, but it was hard for Miriam if she thought I gave more affection to other sisters. I assured her that I wasn't jealous when she was with other guys. That was no help at all. As a result, I began to tire of her emotional struggles.

Journal Entry (March 3, 1978) Miriam and I are going through a rough patch. I feel that I am hardening my heart towards her. I don't want to feel this way. Haven't we hurt each other enough? I wish she would get over it.

To symbolize all the new developments, Mo decided to change the name of our group to "The Family of Love." We were all supposed to tell our parents, *"The Children of God has disbanded!"* I didn't think there was much chance of anyone buying that line, but whatever. I disliked the change and thought "The Family of Love" was a pretty silly name. Lots of Family members shuffled off to new locations, but Miriam and I stayed put as we had been instructed...waiting for Rachel.

Rachel finally made it to Peru in March and came to visit me. She walked into the house looking as gorgeous as ever and greeted me warmly.

"Salem, I have a message for you from Mo and Maria."

"Mo and Maria?"

"Yes. They want to invite you to come live with them. They need a teacher for the children in their household."

I was speechless. To be honest, the first feeling I had was fear. Rachel noticed that I was scrambling for a response.

"Salem, you seem hesitant. Of course, Miriam will come with you."

"It's not that. It's just that I didn't expect such an honor. Do I need to make a decision right now?"

Rachel gave me a knowing look. "Hmm…you're not exactly jumping for joy, are you? But that's fine. Take some time."

"Can Miriam and I have time to think about it?"

"Sure. Just write me when you make up your mind."

That was interesting—Rachel didn't try to talk me into it. In fact, I fancy she was sending me an unspoken message: *Damn right you better think about it.*

IT SEEMED LIKE MY WORK in Peru had been a waste of time.

All my big plans were flushed down the toilet. It stung that I had written all those childcare training materials for nothing. I was also discouraged about my little family—Miriam and Robin. We had been through some tough times. *What was the solution? What were we doing wrong?*

When it came to Mo and Maria's offer, I couldn't get Ezrom out of my mind—if he was a devil, at least he was the devil I knew. And if Ezrom had been kicked out of Mo's household, how long would I last? And then there was our son, Robin, who still required medication. What would Mo say about that? Miriam and I discussed it and decided we would pass on the offer. So I wrote Rachel and told her we preferred to pioneer some new field in South America.

Eventually I got a letter from Rachel saying that Shaul had set up his base in Caracas, Venezuela and would love for us to join him there. I was happy to hear it because I really loved South America. I started to get enthusiastic about going to a new location. I know. I'm really a sucker for "turning over a new leaf." When would I learn? I should have asked myself, *"Had much luck with that, dumbass?"*

We arrived in Caracas on June 7th and were met at the airport by Amminadab, Shiloh and their children. After much hugging and swapping of tales, they took us to our new home in Caracas. It was like a weight had been lifted off me. I was no longer under the pressure of big leadership or big plans. I was hopeful that NOW I would become a new, improved Salem. And then a seductive thought crept up on me from behind. *"Maybe what you need is a REALLY BIG change. Maybe it is time for you and Miriam to split up."*

Amazing what selfish crap you can cook up if you put your mind to it. (When it comes to self-delusion, I'm pretty much an expert.) I flipped through my memory banks and focused on the worst of times. That's always easy. But still, I was not comfortable with the thought of leaving Miriam. I had to find a way to iron out that guilt wrinkle. And this is what I came up with: *"I'm not able to make Miriam happy. So, it's not fair for me to keep her in a painful relationship. I need to release her so she can find someone to meet her needs."* Yeah, that sounded good—just a little twist on the "it's not you, it's me" stance. After presenting this to Miriam, I convinced myself we had come to a mutual decision. I almost felt noble.

So I moved out and wound up at the home where Shaul lived with his wife, Abiah. It was a big house with other married couples, a few children and several single sisters who worked as secretaries and childcare workers. As soon as I arrived, a sister who acted as the colony nurse escorted me to a restroom and asked me to pull down my pants and underwear for a "lice" check. (Lice in quotes because I really think she was checking for STD's.)

After lifting and inspecting my gear, she remarked, "You've got a nice one."

I pulled up my pants and said, "I wish I had a dollar for every time I heard that."

She started laughing. "Oh, you're a funny one."

It wasn't often that people got my sense of humor—so that was appreciated. I was also amused because with my average unit, I knew she told all the guys they had nice ones.

Later I had a meeting with Shaul and Abiah. Their job was to go around South America to confer with colony servants and offer support. Abiah would counsel the sisters, especially those with children. With my childcare background, Shaul wanted me to start travelling around with them. I didn't have a problem with that; but I didn't want to start getting my hopes up for a big childcare ministry (having turned over a new leaf, and all).

I soon settled into the routine and shared kitchen duties, did my share of babysitting, and went out to sell literature regularly. Shaul had a car and occasionally took me with him to visit other Family homes. There were several in the area, like the one Miriam lived in. Amminadab and Shiloh also had a little two-bedroom apartment in town.

The whole setup in Caracas was loosey-goosey with nothing much going on. I think everyone was punch drunk, still processing all the heavy new revolutionary changes. Since this was South America, and everyone had previously been under the rule of Deborah and Jethro, tongues were wagging with gossip about them—especially since Mo had called their leadership a "reign of terror." It's true I had my own reasons for being pissed at Deborah and Jethro; but I thought people were going overboard in their off-with-their-heads fervor.

But then we got the news that Deborah and Jethro had left the Family. That really set Mo off into a hissy fit. He labeled them as backsliding devils and called upon God to kill them. I was a bit conflicted about that. It's true that Deborah had a temper and Jethro could be a jerk; but since I took care of their kids, it put me on their good side. I had learned how to walk through their minefield, only losing a few fingers and toes.

Turns out life without Miriam wasn't exactly the Shangri La I expected. It was strange being all on my own. When I thought of Miriam and Robin, I had a queasy feeling inside. And whenever I visited her to spend time with Robin, I could tell Miriam was sad. However, I tried to push past the heartache and kept up my mantra, *"Miriam is better off without me."* But she didn't seem to be doing better.

After the heavy workload I had in Italy and Peru, Venezuela was a breeze. I often had spare time on my hands. What to do? That problem was soon cleared away. Shaul and Abiah—trying to imitate Mo's household—promoted sexual freedoms amongst Family members. And now I was single.

After 7 years I had grown taller and packed on almost 20 pounds—no longer the string-bean teenager who joined the Family in 1971. Still, I never considered myself to be a chick magnet. So when the girls started asking me to "spend time" with them, I thought it was because they felt sorry for me. *Poor Salem... all alone.* Okay, I didn't put up a fight. I was happy to oblige. New toys always fascinate little boys at first.

But I had a nagging feeling these women wanted more than sex. They wanted attention; they wanted someone to listen to them; they wanted more than I was able to give. That's where things went haywire in our free love environment—there was something missing. Sex, after all, is just meant to be a small portion of your daily life. If you put too much focus on it—delicious as it can be—sex soon loses it's charm.

Being married to just one person is difficult enough; so just imagine living in a large group where everyone is supposed to be married to everyone. I can tell you this: *IT DOESN'T WORK!* Deep down you still long for just one meaningful relationship—not dozens of fairly shallow ones. When you are having sex with everyone, you are making love to no one. It becomes like the quail God sent the Israelites in the wilderness when they lusted after the meat—they ate the quail until it became loathsome to them. That's how I felt. In order to keep up the act, I turned to drink. That was the only way I could handle it. Each time I was called upon to perform with one of the sisters (married or not), I would need to get fairly plastered.

One night Shaul invited all the Family in Caracas to a party. The place got swinging with drinks and music. Suddenly the music stopped and Shaul got everyone to form a circle.

"Listen up. I'm going to show you something I learned at Mo's house. It's a way for us to all enjoy our freedoms together. Mo calls it a COME-UNION. Just keep in mind Mo's teaching: sex is beautiful. Don't be shy about getting naked in front of your Family—that's just pride. Okay, turn the music back on."

Shaul's version of a COME-UNION was an X-rated game of spin the bottle. When the bottle pointed at you, off came your clothes. To start things off, Shaul tapped himself with the bottle and stripped off his clothes to the beat of the music. Then he started undressing the sister closest to him. As they did a naked slow dance, Shaul started to get an erection.

When someone stepped in and continued spinning the bottle, I became extremely uncomfortable. It was obvious we were supposed to follow Shaul's example. Free love was one thing, but an orgy? That took it to a whole different level. I was wondering how to escape when Shaul's wife, Abiah, whispered in my ear.

"Let's get out of here."

"I'm with you."

We went to her room and she opened a bottle of wine. I was surprised when Abiah told me that she really didn't like participating in those games. I had already noticed that Abiah drank a lot. Now I knew why. She was going through the same thing as me. Abiah and I made a pact that we would rescue each other whenever things weren't to our liking. We spent most of the evening talking and drinking and listening to the latest QUEEN album. We must have played "Somebody to Love" a dozen times because it spoke to us: *We did need somebody to love us; each day we were dying little by little.*

I wasn't impressed with Shaul's role as "visiting servant." His answer to any problem was, *"Love, love, love... God's only law is love."* Remember, I was a problem solver and this all-you-need-is-love philosophy sounded weak.

Eventually Mr. Lovey-Dovey Shaul called me in to share some oh-so-helpful suggestions about Robin's convulsions. It was just the same shit I had heard before. But then he surprised me by adding this little juicy bit with his face all wrinkled with righteous concern, *"Have you considered that Robin's attacks might be spiritual? Perhaps he picked up a bad spirit somewhere."*

Do you get it? He was suggesting that Robin might be possessed. This was troubling. I knew the stories well—where Jesus cast demons out of men who had seizures—but it never occurred to me that Robin might have an evil spirit. A little switch flipped in my brain and I thought, *"That's just too damn much! I'm willing to take the blame. Miriam's willing to take the blame. But not our little baby!"* We had tried prayer, soul-searching, confession and repentance of every sin we could think of with no result. Now what? Arrange an exorcism? I was heartsick and confused by our son's condition, but I knew demon possession wasn't the problem.

I believed God had the power to heal. Of course He COULD heal. But WOULD he heal? There's the rub.

And I was damned sick and tired of leaders saying, "What is God trying to teach you?"

I DON'T KNOW! HE'S GOD. I'M NOT. I thought, *"If God wants to send me a message, I wish He would speak up because it seems like I am hard of hearing."* So Shaul actually did me a service by pointing out the obvious—something was wrong with the Family's belief about healing.

After that I pretty much wrote Shaul off as yet another clueless leader. Meanwhile, all the other colony "servants" who had been elected by their various flocks walked around timidly lest they be accused of abusing power. Really, there was no one leading anyone. When I learned to run the kitchen in Detroit, the cook taught me a good lesson:

"You gotta tell people what to do. It's no good expecting them to wash their own dishes. *Everyone's job is NOBODY'S JOB."*

In a few weeks I told Shaul that I wanted to move out of his house. What could he say? It's all about love, baby. I already had a back-up plan. It had become a regular thing for me to go out with Amminadab, Shiloh and their children as they sang in restaurants and on the street. Shiloh always appreciated my help with her kids—quite a lively bunch, I must say. When Amminadab and Shiloh heard I was anxious to escape the quagmire at Shaul's base, they invited me to move in with them. I accepted immediately.

Amminadab shared my misgivings about the Venezuelan non-leadership. Likewise, we were both had some doubts about Mo. We still thought that Mo was a prophet; however, it seemed like his new revolutionary policies were spinning out of control. And now lots of former loyal members were being tossed out of the Family. Even my beloved babe's ranch teacher, Joab, had been excommunicated for disagreeing with Mo. Sheesh! You never knew who was a devil. Who was next? Me?

Amminadab

It was Amminadab who brought up something obvious: almost all the members getting kicked out had originally been placed in positions of authority by Mo himself. What was up with that? Was Mo's prophet ability on the blink back in those days? Wait a minute! The biggest leaders getting the ax—the Royal Family—were Mo's own children. He raised them. Awkward!

I got along well with Amminadab, who was kind of a rock star in the Family, performing for large audiences and even recording albums. He had joined the Children of God way back before Mo started living in secret locations. So Amminadab was full of stories about the glory days. He would also entertain me with little comedy bits where he imitated Mo's voice—sounded just like him, too. He had Mo going on about some crazy new prophecy while fussing at Maria for neglecting to fill his wineglass. (This was just our little inside joke—we knew that other members would consider it blasphemy.)

In October Amminadab, Shiloh and I made plans to exit South America. Our idea was to find a new field to pioneer. I'm not sure how we came up with this, but our destination was Romania. Romania? I don't know, maybe the point was we just wanted to get the hell out of this place.

Journal Entry (October 9, 1978) I am very burdened about Robin. Should I take him with me when we leave? But I think that would freak out Miriam. I think she needs someone to love.

I wanted Robin and Miriam to be taken care of, so for a while I toyed with the idea of getting back together with Miriam. But I doubted our marriage had much chance to survive. Besides, Miriam was royally pissed at me for leaving her in the first place. I didn't think she would even want to come with me. This decision tormented me for weeks.

I know you're probably thinking, *"What a rat! You're thinking about leaving your sick kid in South America?"* Okay, I deserve that. But remember, the doctors told us that Robin had epilepsy, you know, like Julius Caesar. And what can you do about that? You just have to live with it. Then Miriam told me she was invited to move to a new colony and she actually seemed more upbeat, like she was happy about it. *"See there?"* I thought. *"God is working all this out."*

Journal Entry (November 27, 1978) Leaving Miriam and Robin was the hardest decision I ever made. I got this message while I was praying, "Right now you don't understand exactly what is happening, but later you will understand it clearly."

Miriam and the son I left behind.

Before we left South America, I had this really vivid dream. I was in a small boat out in the ocean and I saw a big house floating on the water. I rowed over there and got into the house. As I walked through it, I saw children in one room having school. Then all of a sudden the house started shaking and water was coming up through the floor. I thought, *"This house is sinking. I've got to find someone to help me get these kids out of here."* So, I ran through the house looking for help. I finally came to this little room and saw Mo. But he wouldn't listen to me about the danger. I ran back the way I came—the house was sinking really fast now—and made it just in time to jump out a window. All alone in the ocean, I watched the whole house sink. As I was treading water, I saw my Bible floating on the water. When I reached out to grab it, it sank beneath the surface. I was very upset and dove down to get it; but was so murky I couldn't see much. Then I saw a bright angel way down below, swimming towards me. The angel got to me and handed back my Bible. I started crying with joy. And then I woke up from my dream.

Sometimes when I had a dream that was really heavy, I would wake up with my heart pounding. This was one of those dreams. Somehow I knew this dream was significant. Whatever it meant, I was reminded of my journal entry: *Right now you don't understand exactly what is happening, but later you will understand clearly.*

It was almost the end of 1978 and I spent a week making the rounds and saying my farewells to brothers and sisters in Caracas. Then on December 9, Amminidab, Shiloh and I, along with their kids, boarded a plane headed for Texas.

Once in the air, we were all in a jovial mood. The stewardess started serving drinks and passing out magazines. I accepted both and was handed a Coke and the latest Time magazine. It was the December 4th edition. Splashed all over the cover was the caption: CULT OF DEATH! The stories inside detailed an event that was news to me: the Jonestown mass suicide. I read and reread all the articles with growing alarm. My spider-sense was tingling like crazy...

I closed the magazine and muttered, *"Well, fuck me!"*

10

December 1978 to February 1994

Rapunzel, Rapunzel, let down your hair
I want to return to your hidden lair
Please let me in and I'll never go astray
But the woman sighed and refused to obey

LIFE AFTER THE END OF THE WORLD

IN THE FAMILY WE ALL knew about a guy named Ted Patrick.
He was a deprogrammer parents would hire to get their kids out of cults. There were stories of how he would kidnap cult members off the street and hold them against their will until they listened to sense. I used to indulge in sweet daydreams of being snatched by Ted Patrick and standing strong against all his attacks. That's funny because in the end all it took was a magazine article to blow my house down.

By the time our plane landed in Houston, I had shared the *Time* magazine article with Amminadab and Shiloh. We all felt queasy about the implications. Our plan was to meet up after Christmas before embarking on our grand pioneer scheme. I sure needed some time to think things over. My sister, who lived in the area, said I could crash at her place for a while. I spent the next few weeks in a state of mental disarray.

I couldn't get over the pictures of all the bodies around those pots of Kool-Aid. Was the Family a cult like Jonestown? Had I been wrong about everything? Had I been right about anything? As usual, I used my journal to deal with the bull in the china shop of my head.

Journal Entry (December 19, 1978) I don't know what to do. I wanted a way to serve the Lord and I found the Children of God. The Family got me off drugs and I learned lots about the Bible. But now Mo claims his words are more important than the Bible. That really bugs me. I think God used Mo in the beginning, but now I'm

not so sure.

After a few weeks I thought of Ezrom. He had spent time at Mo's house. Maybe he could give me a firsthand report on the Prophet. Ezrom was originally from Texas, so he had probably landed back here. I actually knew his real name and what town he came from. With the help of a friendly telephone information lady, it didn't take long for me to track him down. I recognized his familiar voice as soon as he answered his phone.

"Ezrom, this is Salem. I just came back to Texas from South America."

"Salem? Man, I never thought I'd hear from you again. Are you still in the Family?"

"Can't say. I'm kind of in limbo now. Can I talk to you about it?"

"I can give you an earful, buddy."

"Lay it on me."

"Here's the thing—Mo is nothing like what you read in his letters. He's drunk most of the time. His wives try to control his drinking, but it is hard to refuse the great prophet."

"Did you say wives?"

"Hell, yes. He's got a collection of them there at his house. He calls them his *queens*."

"What happened with your wife, Cedar?"

"Between her sleeping with Mo and other guys, I saw less and less of her. It bummed me out. And then Mo rebuked me for having a *jealous spirit*. I don't know how it was where you were, but at Mo's house there were not supposed to be any private marriages. Let me tell you, it was a drag."

"That happened to me in Venezuela. I went to bed with lots of sisters, but didn't feel connected to anyone."

"Okay, Salem, you get it. And then there was 'Flirty Fishing.' Mo was big into that. He sent the girls out to nightclubs to find the *big fish*. That's what paid the rent."

"Wasn't the goal to show God's love? Did any of these guys ever join the Family?"

"From what I saw, most of them were just after the sex. But Mo was convinced this would be the start of something big. When he took the girls out to the clubs, he was all decked out like a prophet with his long beard and this cloak he liked to wear. Then he would sit at a table and watch the flirty fishing action."

"I suppose that meant more drinking."

"That's for sure. One night he got really shit-faced and told me to go find him a prostitute. When I told him I wouldn't do it, man, was he pissed."

"Why would he need a prostitute?"

"I know, right? I'm telling you. Mo is a sex junkie. And no one dares to question his judgments. I got tired of his bullshit and told everyone how I felt, that it seemed like a racket. After that, of course, I had to go."

"Miriam and I were invited to work at Mo's house. But we turned down the offer because I knew you had been kicked out. I didn't want the same thing to happen to me."

"Salem, you really dodged a bullet there. At least you're thinking things over now. My advice? Get out and stay out!"

Ezrom gave me some important information, but I still wavered. Why wasn't it enough? I was fighting against eight years of deeply engrained thought patterns and habits. It was hard to let go of the support system that gave me significance. I had most of the puzzle pieces now, but I didn't want to betray Jesus. Maybe there was a way to hang onto the Family's core beliefs, but on my own—kind of like a Lone Ranger. I could almost hear Bob Dylan singing "Like A Rolling Stone" because I felt alone, no longer with any direction to go in.

I already missed the fellowship of the group. But more than that, I missed Miriam and Robin. As I reviewed my bad decisions, I realized I had really blown it with Miriam. But how could I get her back? Was it too late?

Whenever I visited Amminadab and Shiloh, no one even mentioned Romania. Instead, we spent hours talking things over, trying to hash things out. I knew I had to make a choice. One day I took a long walk and wound up in a park. I just sat under a tree for most of the day, going back and forth. Was the Family right or wrong? Should I stay in or get out?

By now I knew better than to ask God to "tell me" what to do. I didn't trust special revelations anymore. That hocus-pocus had not served me well. But I did ask God to help me make up my mind. It was dark when I walked back to my sister's house. With much fear and trembling I called Amminadab.

"I'm quitting the Children of God."

"Salem, that's funny. Shiloh and I just decided the same thing."

Journal Entry (January 5, 1979) The Family started out doing some good but lost its way. Maybe God put me through it because I had some things to learn. Seems like a hard way to learn lessons. Now I have to pick up where I left off.

I DIDN'T WANT TO KEEP mooching off my sister forever.

So I had to commit the unpardonable sin—at least in the Family's estimation—and get a job. I looked through the newspaper want ads. There were lots of telemarketing jobs available, but that seemed like a drag. I interviewed at a couple of daycare centers (slightly less dismal). But then I found a Montessori school nearby. It was the middle of the school year, so I knew they wouldn't be hiring teachers; but I called anyway and asked if they could use a classroom assistant. The school director told me they did need some help in the afternoons to handle something called "after school care." After an interview, with my Montessori background, I was hired right away.

Miriam and I still exchanged letters. She mentioned she would be visiting her father at the end of January. That's all I needed to know. My Plan A was to meet Miriam in Alabama and try to talk her out of the Family. If that didn't work I'd shift to Plan B and ask her to let me take Robin so that he could see another doctor. I didn't know if Miriam would go for it, but it was worth a shot.

I flew up to Alabama to meet Miriam, not knowing how she would react. After all, it took me weeks to make my own decision to leave the Family. So I prepared a soft approach: *MAYBE David Berg started off as our shepherd, but what about now? There were many good things about the Family, but what about now?* I had a whole page of notes prepared with arguments.

I was so happy to see Miriam and Robin. I played it cool at first, but when Robin went down for his nap, I went ahead with my pitch. The Jonestown massacre was a good start, especially since all the victims were convinced they were following God's prophet. Miriam hadn't heard all the details about the mass suicide and was horrified. Then I eased into my conversation with Ezrom. Was I making some headway? At least Miriam wasn't freaking out and holding up a crucifix.

I begged Miriam to leave the group even if it was just to take some time off. But I think I moved too fast.

"Salem, you've given me some things to think about. But I can't leave the Family right away."

"Why not?"

"I'm in a relationship with the South American representative of General Electric. He's a big fish and supports the Family where I live. If I quit, that support will be cut off. I can't let the Family down like that."

Even with the shocking things I had revealed to her, Miriam still felt loyalty to the Family. So I shifted the conversation to our son. How was he doing? Were his seizures getting any worse? What kind of care did he get when she was away from the home. I could see some cracks. Of course, Miriam was concerned about Robin's health and welfare. She had to admit that things were not so great for him.

"Miriam, if you let me take Robin back to Texas, he could attend the Montessori school where I work. Houston has a famous medical center. I could have him checked out and get a second opinion. Maybe there's something doctors can do to improve his condition."

"I'm not sure what to do. Maybe it would be better for Robin to be with you."

Miriam was wavering, but I had no more arguments. So I told her about the dream I had about Mo's house sinking in the ocean. Somehow that impressed Miriam and she finally gave in. The next day I flew back to Texas with Robin, leaving a tearful mommy behind. I knew it was hard for her; but I was convinced that if I had Robin, Miriam would soon follow.

Robin missed his mother terribly, but eventually settled into his new situation. Now, instead of sending letters, I called Miriam on the phone so she could speak to Robin. Under that guise, I could check where she was at in her thinking. Robin and I moved into an apartment and as I promised, he attended the Montessori preschool.

I did manage to find a respected clinic in the medical center so Robin could get reevaluated. The doctors put him through all the tests he had been given in South America, including a CT scan—something that was not available at the Peruvian hospital. I was optimistic the American doctors could find something that had been missed. But when all the results were in, the conclusion was the same. Apart from seizure activity, nothing out or the ordinary was detected—no brain injury, tumor or deformity. As before, I was told anticonvulsant medication was the only option. The only ray of hope was that there were new drugs that might prove more effective.

I just had to accept it. At least I had done all I could to find a medical solution. So I moved on and focused on my job and being a single dad. When the school year ended I was hired to do a summer session at the Montessori school. That meant more pay. Things were looking up—or so you would think. Truth is, I still struggled with life out of the group.

Many Children of God practices were second nature to me. No matter where we went, we always shared to Gospel with any warm body we met. Waiting in line? Share the Gospel. Riding on a bus? Witness to the person next to you. Everyone was a prospective convert. We always had to be busy with God's work. I might have been out of the Family, but these habits exerted constant pressure on me. I also had doubts and fears about where I stood with God. How could I sort it all out? It was like trying to unravel a mile long string of tangled Christmas tree lights.

Journal Entry (June 22, 1979) Sometimes I feel on the verge of collapse because of my spiritual emptiness. I try to get comfort from the Bible, but it gives me nothing. I'm tempted to pack it away as a useless relic. Is there nothing that can be salvaged from the beliefs I once held dear?

Mo had no qualms about tossing out pieces of the Bible. When he was done, there was not much left. But I held onto the Bible like a talisman, thinking that some day its power might be restored. I had no such qualms about the Mo Letters. I had a suitcase full of them and they made a nice little bonfire. I was tempted to toss in all my journal booklets and notes, but decided against it at the last minute.

One day I got a surprise call from Deborah. How she got my number is still a mystery.

"Salem, this is Deborah. Are you doing okay?"

"Deborah! Wow! Where are you?"

"I'm in California with all my children. But I wanted to call and tell you something. I'm so sorry for all I put you through in Italy and South America. The Family made lots of mistakes and I should have left a long time ago. But, well, David Berg is my father and it was hard. Still, I'm sorry. Will you forgive me?"

"Gosh, Deborah, I don't know what to say. I guess I do, forgive you, I mean. I decided not to go back to the Family. It wasn't an easy decision and I'm still confused about lots of things."

"I know what you're going through. It's been hard on all of us. Salem, what about Miriam?"

"She's still in the Family in Venezuela. But I have Robin here with me."

"You really need to get her out. Things will only get worse. I can assure you of that. My father has let all this power go to his head."

"I met with her in Alabama and tried to talk her out of the group. But she went back to South America anyway."

"I can tell you some things that might help you."

After listening to what Deborah had to say, I was really anxious to get Miriam out of the Family. Whenever I called her it was very hush-hush because she would be cross-examined about our conversations. Miriam was told not listen to me. But since I had Robin, what could they do? They couldn't cut her off from her child.

"Miriam, don't tell anyone...but...I got a call from Deborah."

"Deborah? What did she have to say?"

"First off, she actually apologized for things she had done in the Family. And she told me stuff I think you ought to hear."

"Okay, I'm alone now. Tell me."

"You know all the stuff about sexual freedom? We all thought it was a new revelation from Mo. But he has practiced it for a long time."

"Salem, I kind of figured that out already. I mean…he was sleeping with Maria."

"Actually, Mo started fooling around before Maria. And he passed down his sexual liberties to all his top leadership."

Miriam paused. "Well, that's a new one. I thought the Family was so sexually pure in the beginning—just husbands and wives, you know."

"I know. Deborah told me Mo justified it by saying he was an exception to the rules. And here's a shocker—he abused Faithy."

"What? He had sex with his own daughter?"

"Yes. Deborah said he tried it on her, but she resisted him."

"Salem, this is pretty hard to take. Why in the world did she stay in the Family?"

"Deborah said we don't know how persuasive her father can be. Deborah had doubts, but Mo always came up with Bible verses that seemed to support what he did. And when so many people joined the Family, Deborah was convinced it was a great movement of God."

"Hold on, Salem… someone came in the room… okay, go on. They left."

"Miriam, did you ever meet Deborah's brother, Aaron?"

"Sure, he was in London when I was there. Then later we heard he had an accident in the Alps while hiking and was killed."

"It was no accident. Aaron committed suicide. He was very disillusioned with the Family. His wife found the suicide note in his bedroom."

"Salem, we were never told anything like that."

"Of course not. It was a closely guarded secret."

"I have to think about all this."

"Be careful. If they find out what I told you, they won't let me call anymore."

IT WASN'T LONG BEFORE MIRIAM decided to leave the Family.

This was just what I hoped would happen. I was very excited when she asked if I could pick her up at the Houston airport. Would God put us back together again? I had high hopes. When Miriam arrived, Robin was so happy to see her. For a while we were a happy family again.

It didn't last long. After a few days I told Miriam I loved her and hoped we could reunite as a married couple. I gave her a big kiss and pulled back to get her reaction. It wasn't what I expected.

Miriam shook her head and said, "I'm sorry. I know you are trying hard. But I don't feel that way about you anymore."

"I thought we could be together again."

"No, I don't think it would work."

This hit me hard, but I didn't push it. At least Miriam and Robin were out of the Family. So I let it go. Maybe it was for the best. After all, our relationship had quite a history of rejection. We got married and Miriam had regrets. By the time she changed her mind about me, my heart had grown cold. Finally I split up with her in South America. So now it was Miriam's turn to ax my plan for reconciliation. She had enough of me.

Miriam eventually got her own apartment and bounced around from job to job. She worked at a nursing home, then at a local newspaper, and then at a sandwich shop. She even became a nanny for a while. In the end Miriam and I became friends. Robin spent most of his days with me since he went to my school; but Miriam saw him often and took him for weekends.

Before the 1979-1980 school year began, I was invited to become a full-time teacher at the Montessori School. Meanwhile, I rekindled a relationship with an old girlfriend and things heated up fast. We even talked about marriage—a new wife for my new life. I was running for the cliff's edge chanting, *"The girl of my dreams. I'm going to be so happy!"* But before that could happen, I had to get a divorce. Miriam had no problem with it since she was living with another guy. I spoke to my father, the lawyer, and he said he would start the divorce proceedings whenever we were ready.

Meanwhile, I tracked down Paul Bunyan who now lived in Minnesota with his wife and three children. When we spoke on the phone it was like we never had any problems getting along. We spent many hours discussing our exits from the Family, how we had handled it and where we were now headed. While my faith dwindled, Paul's was rekindled. He talked about how he and his wife had marital difficulties but prayed about it and decided to stay together.

Paul was disappointed that Miriam and I were getting a divorce and urged me to reconsider. I explained that Miriam wanted to move on. Besides, I had a new relationship. Still, I'll have to admit, Paul's words kind of shook me up. Had I given up too easily when Miriam rejected the idea of us getting back together? And then there was my girlfriend. My relationship with her filled me with all the new-car-smell excitements a young man could hope for. Give that up? It seemed like too much to ask.

In the summer of 1980 I was headhunted by another, larger Montessori school. Even though it involved a move, their offer was too good for me to pass up. Instead of looking for another apartment, I bought an Airstream trailer and set up shop in a trailer park. That would make for an easy move. Miriam, not wanting to live far from Robin, asked if she could move in with us. She said after we relocated, she would find her own place. I'm sure folks thought we were kind of kooky—about to get divorced but still living together.

Then I got something in the mail from Paul Bunyan: a ticket to a Christian seminar. Sounded like church and I wasn't interested. But when I offered the ticket to Miriam, she decided to go. I was surprised because, like me, Miriam had pretty much stopped reading the Bible. I told myself, *"Maybe it will do her some good and pull her out of a slump."* And off she went to a weeklong series of lectures. The results couldn't have been more shocking.

I was stunned when Miriam announced she wanted to get back together with me, convinced that God would restore our marriage. What? Come on—a little late for that, don't you think? What had I done, letting her go off and get her head turned about? (And, by the way, thanks a lot Paul Bunyan!) I flat out refused to consider it. I was on the path to remarriage and wasn't about to retrace my steps and pick up where we left off. But Miriam was adamant. In fact, she proclaimed that even if I divorced her, she would remain faithful to me and never to marry another man. Sheesh! I just hoped her ardor would fade with time.

That summer Miriam and I relocated and I geared up for the new school year. Miriam was well behaved, but kept up her campaign to win me back. Nevertheless, I continued making plans with my girlfriend. (She lived in another city but would visit me occasionally). Then, in August of

1980, we heard that the powerful Hurricane Allen was coming our way. Besides the high winds and rain, tornadoes were a possibility. Fearful that the Airstream would be damaged, I left Miriam and Robin safely with friends and hauled the trailer inland. I barely got out of town before all hell broke loose.

There I was, alone in the storm, with wild winds and rain buffeting the trailer. With no electricity, I only had candles to give me light. Since I would be stuck for a couple of days, I looked around for something to read. Slim pickings, but I did come across the workbook Miriam brought back from her Christian seminar. I thought, *"Well, I'll just check this out to see what's up with Miriam."* It was filled with notes on various subjects, mostly dealing with conflicts young Christian encounter.

Some of the lectures addressed things I was going through and offered good advice. I had to admit, *"Hey! This is not so bad."* And so for hours I reviewed all this material. It was almost like I had attended the seminar with Miriam. Things were rolling along nicely until I came across the lectures on marriage and divorce. Uh oh! This was dangerous, rattle-my-cage territory. What hit me hard was that most of the instructions were from the lips of Jesus—the one I loved before joining the Children of God.

When the skies cleared, I drove back home with a different storm raging in my head. Was I doing the right thing, divorcing Miriam? My confidence was besieged and all my calculations seemed fuzzy. While Miriam was delighted to hear I was reconsidering my position, I was quite gloomy. So she tamped down her enthusiasm and let me work it out. It took me days to make up my mind—several dark days. But it was like Jesus put his arm around my shoulder and said, "Friend, follow me."

The phone call to my girlfriend was one of the hardest things I have ever done. She was crying and begged to see me in person before I finalized my decision. But I knew I could never do that. I was too weak. She told me it wasn't fair—we had such wonderful plans. It was very heartbreaking, but I told her I had to give my marriage one more chance.

Okay, so, Miriam and Salem back together again. And they lived happily ever after. The End. No, it was not a nice fairy tale ending. We both had many wounds that would require time to heal. Miriam got what she wanted, but now had to deal with my melancholy. She would have to carry the burden of doubt about my commitment for quite some time.

But the truth was—even though I didn't feel like a loving husband—I knew I was doing the right thing. I felt hopeless, but still had hope.

Miriam and I had been lost in the woods after the birds ate our breadcrumbs. With the taste of the witch's candy house still in our mouths, we now had to make our way through the dark and find our way home. Miriam and I had loved each other before, just not always at the same time. Our marriage was like the stock market going up and down—bull market, bear market, recession, and depression. Could we ever expect an upswing?

I did well at my new school. Miriam and I traded in our trailer for a mobile home and could almost pass as a normal married couple—as long as we kept quiet about our weird backstory. Sometimes we got along and sometimes we bickered (typical married stuff). And then there was our son. While he benefited from having mom and dad together, it became clear that Robin had more than a seizure disorder. We could tell he was developmentally delayed. Were the convulsions causing it or was it all the medication we gave him? One pharmacist told me it was enough to knock out a horse.

My father heard about an operation where surgeons go in and remove the seizure focal point from the brain. It sounded scary, but we thought it was worth exploring. I took some time off and we flew Robin up to the Mayo clinic in April of 1983. After a day of medical testing, the doctors came to us and said, "Who told you this was epilepsy? Your son has a brain tumor the size of an orange."

Miriam and I were stunned. Many good doctors and neurologists had examined Robin, but none of them got it right. The tumor had been present since birth and had grown slowly, eventually causing brain damage. While we waited for the surgery to be scheduled, I wandered the hospital corridors and finally came upon a small chapel room. I fell into one of the chairs and sobbed, "Robin, my son. Oh, my poor son, Robin."

The operation took several hours and was followed by a very long recovery. While I was relieved we knew the cause of Robin's seizures, on another level I was disturbed.

"Why, God, why? Why couldn't we have found out sooner?"

(no answer)

"Well, I guess that fills up my lifetime tragedy quota."

(no answer)

Having been zapped by lightning, I felt safe—like I had endured enough suffering. After such a dramatic event, I dared to hope that Robin would get better now. Back in Texas we took him to a specialist to be evaluated.

Then the doctor interviewed us and asked us "What kind of future do you expect for your son?"

I replied, "I'd just be happy if he learned a trade and settled down in a mobile home with a plump little Mexican wife."

"That's an unusual answer. Haven't heard it before. And hope is good. But I don't think you know what you are in for."

Although Robin's tumor was successfully removed, he was left with a weakness on his left side, impaired vision, learning difficulties, and—at the top of the list—and acute case of obsessive-compulsive disorder. Although we tried putting him in a Montessori class, it was never a good fit. Robin needed all kinds of extra help.

We had no choice but to enroll him in public school to take advantage of their special education program. Ah, public school—the gift that keeps on giving—where the general population would shun Robin and where he would be taunted by bullies. As anyone with a disabled kid can testify, you just try to keep your head above the water and deal with things as they come your way.

Journal Entry (June 6, 1983) I'm like Robin. I need to have the tumor in my own head removed—the cancerous bitterness, anger and frustration about the past. Is it symbolic? Can we both heal now?

ONE THING ABOUT MIRIAM, SHE'S always full of surprises.

She decided to enroll in a Montessori training course and, after much study, became a certified teacher herself. As a result, she was able to find employment in all the schools where I worked. Meanwhile I decided to take as many college courses as I could while teaching fulltime. As I moved my wife and kid from one city to another—being lured by better, higher paying teaching positions—I plugged into whatever community colleges or universities were available. It took me eight years of night school, Saturday classes and summer sessions to earn my bachelor's degree (the same amount of time I spent in the cult).

But now I had a college degree and a moderate income from a job I was pretty good at. We even purchased a house and moved into middleclass suburbia. You would think things were looking up for me. But I knew there was a hole—I no longer had a spiritual calling. In the Children of God we believed we had an awesome mission because, obviously, we worked for the Big Boss who passed out rewards in heaven. Even though that whole deal was flushed down the toilet, I still wondered if God would replace it with something better. But nothing materialized.

In an effort to fill up the void, I threw myself into my profession. It didn't take long before most of my time was dedicated to teaching. My job became the big thing in my life and that's where I blew it. My cause was education and it took precedence over everything. It was my new cult. I was usually the first one at the school and the last one to leave. My weekends and summers were also gobbled up. It seemed like I couldn't help myself. The years rolled by and I just got busier.

It's not that I didn't know better. I wanted very much to slow down. But I kept telling myself, "I'll take it easy when I get (blank) done." But when (blank) got done there was always another (blank) to take its place. Meanwhile, I was writing in my journal like crazy, trying to reach a point of clarity, trying to fill a bottomless pit. However, I could never shovel in enough dirt. I was feverishly working at it when 1994 rolled around.

And then came the breakdown.

11

February 1994 to December 1996

Foolish Jack met a man and fell for his schemes
Traded all he had for some magical beans
Jack ran away from the giant's dining room
But the monster followed him, threatening doom

GETTING INTO THE WEEDS

I WAS HAVING A TERRIBLE nightmare and woke up with a start. My heart was beating wildly and it felt like a weight was on my chest. When I got out of bed, I was dizzy and fell to the floor. My left arm felt numb and my head tingled.

It came to me, *"So this is what it is like to die."*

Miriam hurried to my side. "What's wrong?"

"Call 911. I think I'm having a heart attack."

The ambulance arrived quickly and whisked me away to the hospital. By that time I was experiencing tunnel vision and the ride was like a bad drug trip. In the ER they took my vitals, put me in a gown and got the party started.

During the next few hours my symptoms faded away, then returned, then disappeared again. What the hell was going on? For the next few days I was put through a variety of examinations and medical tests. In the end there was a general consensus: they could find nothing wrong with me. So I was discharged without a clue.

I went to bed the next night thankful it hadn't been anything serious. And then—wham! I woke up at 3 AM with the exact same symptoms. This time I made it to the living room and decided to tough it out. I paced back and forth, hoping it would pass quickly. It didn't. At 6:00 in the morning my distress had faded into exhaustion. Then it was time to get ready for work.

This kept happening almost every night. During my worst spells I was convinced I was losing my mind. Days turned into weeks with no relief. My family doctor finally referred me to a specialist, a funny little fellow everyone called Dr. L. As I gave my blow-by-blow-no-detail-left-out story he interrupted me.

"I get the picture. You're having panic attacks," he said.

"Wha...panic attacks? Are you sure?"

"Yes, I'm sure. Your symptoms are quite common."

"But why would I start having panic attacks?

Dr. L looked over his glasses at me and said, "Just lucky, I guess."

That was his unique bedside manner. Dr. L went on to explain that something was messing with my brain chemistry, *flipping on the fight or flight switch* and triggering a cascade of powerful hormones. In an emergency situation, like being attacked by an escaped gorilla, this reaction is just what you need. But in my case, the gorilla was all in my head.

Dr. L put me on some anti-anxiety medication and that helped. But the pills also caused me to gain 20 pounds and made me feel like a neutered tomcat. Still, it was better than getting up at the witching hour— 3 AM every morning. After a few months Dr. L. suggested another medication with a shorter list of side effects. Then he gave me a little piece of wisdom:

"It helps to know what's happening in your body. That flood of anxiety doesn't actually indicate danger. You may feel like you're dying, but really, you aren't."

That turned out to be useful information. Whenever an attack came and my mind freaked out, I held onto the hope that it would pass. Experience taught me the anticipatory signals of an episode so I could distract myself from falling off the panic cliff.

So how about that? I've got something wrong with me! I'm diagnosed with an actual disorder and have to take medication.

This new reality threw me into a negative feedback loop and slowly drained away my enthusiasm and energy. I felt bummed out at work, bummed out at home, and bummed out being alive. I just wanted to withdraw. Depression slowly crept up behind me, got a good hold, and body slammed me to the ground.

I may have learned how to talk myself down from a panic attack, but depression didn't play so nice. It was a different kind of beast. It wanted to do all the talking and didn't like to be interrupted. Panic attacks made me feel like I was dying; but depression made me wish I were dead. Not a good state of mind when you're supposed to be a happy-happy teacher.

As the melancholy got worse, I switched to a half-day work schedule. But depression works full time, 24 hours a day, 7 days a week. Eventually I quit work altogether and spent most of my time on a couch, napping or watching television. Depression shades the way you look at yourself. Your failures are blown out of proportion. And even your successes seem worthless, like you were just faking it all along.

This was out of Dr. L's league, so he suggested a mental health specialist. And that's how I entered my psychiatrist period. While psychiatrists are usually warm, smiley guys—and several have treated me—they are mainly drug pushers with a goal of matching a pill to your problem. The first medication I was given didn't work, so I tried another one. Kind of worked, but not a silver bullet. It was months before I found something to take the edge off. However, anti-depressants—and I thank God for them—didn't turn out to be magic pills. They did give me some breathing space, and even helped me think straight (well, straighter), but I still had some dark days.

As I worked through all this, I received pep talks and advice from lots of people. One of my co-workers at school said, "You were such a dedicated and enthusiastic teacher. Don't you think you'd feel better if you returned to the classroom? You could focus on the children. You wouldn't have time to get depressed."

And how did I respond? *"You just don't get it. It's not just that I want to stop teaching. I want to have NEVER taught."*

That summed up my mental state—all my hopes and dreams sucked into a black hole.

A concerned Christian friend came by to check up on me. I tried to describe the visceral, mind-tearing experience of my panic attacks (something I discovered to be a useless exercise since panic attacks are almost indescribable).

He put his hand on my shoulder. "You should have just cried out to the Lord for help."

I just shook my head. "There is no God in panic attacks."

Those words shocked me (and I think it almost burned this guy's ears off). But I meant that I felt abandoned with no help to be had. In the middle of an attack it was like I had rocks in my head, grinding against

235

each other, noisily drowning out my prayers.

When I, like an idiot, went on to talk about my depression, my friend was perplexed. (Bewilderment is the standard first response coming from those who haven't been through depression.) So my comforter decided I needed some frank spiritual counsel to snap me out of it.

"Where's your faith? You have Jesus. What do you have to be depressed about? Just fight through it!"

Okay, so he meant well. Not his fault. He didn't know I was struggling in the faith arena. When the depression hit me, I tried hard to keep up my Bible reading, but it seemed like I was just going through the motions, like I was only performing a superstitious ritual—a daily dose of the Bible to ward off evil spirits. So after a while I gave it up. Perhaps part of me decided that since I was such a mess it would be a hypocritical sham to keep it up. I no longer felt whole. Something integral had been ripped away and in my grief I was whispering: *Lord, I've lost it. The spark. The inspiration. You'll have to give it back to me.* Then I stopped praying altogether. If I had faith, it was a faintly burning ember.

I WAS GLUED TO MY couch for months, licking my wounds.

Then a friend told me about something called *cognitive therapy*—an approach designed to help people with mood disorders. So I dragged myself to the bookstore and found a volume on the subject. I flipped through the pages for a while just to make sure it wasn't a load of *think-positive-and-hang-in-there* crap. Didn't seem that way, written by a psychiatrist and all. So, what the hell, I bought a copy.

The basic concept of cognitive therapy is pretty simple: *Thinking influences feeling.* That makes sense, right? I already knew my state of mind gave me distorted perceptions. But would the techniques in the book help me to examine my thoughts and separate the real from the irrational? I'll admit I was doubtful at first. It seemed like I was already agonizing over my thoughts way too much, endlessly going over them like a snake eating its tail. But then I remembered good old Dr. L who told me something was screwing up my brain's wiring. Obviously, he was correct. So decided cognitive therapy was worth a try.

Here's how it went. First I had to identify a bothersome thought—something that got me down. Then came the therapeutic twist. I had to challenge the validity of the negative message. It was like finding a cognitive cavity, drilling it out and getting a more realistic filling—*mental hygiene*. It was a slow process, especially at first. After all, some of my knee-jerk reactions were like ingrained habits. It wasn't an instant cure, but as I kept chipping away at it—slowly, oh so slowly—I saw some cracks in the bricks of my depression prison.

For sure, the medication did help. Without it I never would have had the mental energy to explore cognitive therapy. As I worked through the steps, it became clear I had lots of anxiety inducing obstacles to overcome. Of course there were the usual suspects: disappointment, failure, guilt and stress. Those are all huge, of course; but the big thing with me was the thought that I had failed God.

The Children of God put a lot of pressure on its members to be righteous (at least their form of righteousness). No surprise, right? We were always being watched by the leaders to see if we were behaving like true revolutionary disciples. Eight years of that left me with the conviction that if I worked hard at being good then I'd be rewarded with peace and happiness. God would be pleased and I'd no longer be tormented by emotions, doubts or bad behavior. All I needed—pay close attention here—was to just get serious about it, to make up my mind not to make mistakes!

Out of the Family, I tried to change my behavior. My attempts were usually short-lived. I still thought I could make a fresh start by the force of my will. *I will stop pouting when I get mad at my wife. I will stop bitching about my boss. I will stop my surreptitious drinking. I will stop…(insert bad habit here).* I guess you could say my model was Ebenezer Scrooge. I wanted to have an "AHA!" moment where my heart was changed and "God bless us everyone!" But—"Bah! Humbug"—I always fell short. I kept trying to climb up that steep hill of perfection, only to tumble back down in humiliation. And then my depression mocked me. "Face it, loser! You're kind of bad at being good."

I felt like Homer Simpson in the episode where a little devil is on one of his shoulders arguing with a little angel on the other shoulder. But my little devil was very clever and my little angel seemed kind of slow. When I pounded down one bad behavior, two others popped up—like whack-a-mole.

My goodness waxed and waned like the moon. When it was a dim crescent, I fretted over my blunders, past and present. It's good to learn from your mistakes, but guilt is like quicksand if you don't watch out. The Children of God used guilt to keep us all in line. They cooked up a hot dish of self-flagellation, seasoned well with uptight introspection and served on a bed of unrealistic expectations. I ate up all that junk and now had a serious case of food poisoning. I had been out of the Family for years, but a lingering residue of that indoctrination clung to me.

You don't have to join a cult to scoop up programming like that; but that's where I picked it up. As code writers say, garbage in/garbage out—and I had lots of bad code to be deleted and rewritten. There were deep things still driving me—driving me crazy. And that was a big slice of my depression. I felt cut off from God with nothing to show for my life. I could picture Jesus saying, "What a disappointment you turned out to be!"

Antidepressants and cognitive therapy tricks steered me away from the edge. But did I feel back to normal? Not by a long shot. You know how people have a bad accident and have to learn to walk again? That's how I was mentally—pretty shaky. I had this vague unease, you know, like I was halfway to Europe on the plane and couldn't shake the feeling I'd missed something. Did I turn off the oven? Did I leave Kevin home alone?

I FOUGHT AGAINST MY DEMONS without calling upon God.

With my long history of faults and major screw-ups, I was basically hiding from him. What did God think of me now? Did he still love me? Was I still his child? But one day I thought of my own child, my brain damaged son. Did I still love him, handicaps and all? Of course I did. Did I stop caring for him because of his condition? Absolutely not! In fact, his problems require even more care from me. It came to me, *"Maybe that's how it is between God and me."*

Then I remembered my first encounter with God while on LSD—a somewhat unorthodox entry to faith. It's like my trip had been interrupted. *"And now a message from your sponsor."* God's presence and his loving communication filled me with indescribable joy. And if it had merely been the result of a mind-altering drug, wouldn't it have faded away to nothing? But my friends and family saw a sudden change in me and were puzzled. I had a mind shift and went from doubt to faith—and not just belief in God, but belief in a loving God. That's actually what caused me to lose interest in drugs. I replaced them with prayer—something that expanded my mind more than any psychedelic. I had to conclude that God used the once-in-a-lifetime experience to get through to me—like a jumpstart.

I realized that depression had knocked me off the path. I had shut myself off from God while fighting the battle on my own. So maybe it was time to look to a higher power. There was my old Bible sitting on the bookshelf gathering dust. It had been quite a while; but I had this longing inside like an aching hunger. That book had given me comfort and peace of mind for decades and yet I had pushed it aside. Why? And then it came to me: I was pissed off…not at God, but at myself. I was furious that I was not able to stay up on the pedestal I had so carefully crafted. Failing to live up to my own grand expectations, my depression was a form of self-punishment. And wounded pride, my friends, is a harsh taskmaster.

Could I get back my love for the Bible? There was only one way to find out. But where should I start? Why not return to the Gospel of John, the first book I read back in 1970? And as I read again, I experienced a familiar tug on my heart because the person it described, Jesus, was worthy of my love. The words of Jesus were wonderful, delightful, even overwhelming me to the point of tears. I knew he loved me and I loved him back. His story was convincing—not like a myth or legend. Jesus was real, more real than me—that's for sure. And as I basked in his teachings, the fog began to clear. I still loved Jesus, my heart's desire. I felt like the officers who were sent to arrest Christ, but returned empty-handed.

"Why didn't you bring him in?" the priests demanded.

The officers confessed, "No man ever spoke like this man."

I knew what my father would say. *"What? You went through all that religious nonsense and you're still reading the Bible? It seems like you would have gotten it out of your system. I thought you were smarter than that."*

Clinical depression had pushed me into a kind of dead zone. In that state of mind, my former religious affections seemed inextricably tangled with the cult experience. My melancholy caused me to doubt what I once held dear and I came close to abandoning my faith. But as I emerged from the dark night, my hope in God began to rise.

Then I remembered the dream I had right before breaking away from the Children of God. *The house where David Berg lived collapsed into the ocean and I barely escaped the wreckage. While I was thrashing about in the water, my Bible slipped from my hands and disappeared. But as I mourned the loss, an angel swam up and placed it back in my hands.* That's one dream come true. I had been knocked about by waves of depression and was almost pulled under. And the Bible had been pulled out of my hands for a while. Now it was returned into my outstretched hands.

It wasn't an overnight transformation. It took a while to move from spiritual stagnancy to a restoration of my Bible reading habits—like exercising atrophied muscles. But clearly, something was different. Reading the Bible was no longer merely a daily ritual to check off my good-boy list. It was much more than that: it was my necessary food, my nourishment. It was the ultimate cognitive therapy.

The Bible speaks to me about the human condition. I have no problem accepting the reality of sin. And I don't even have to trot out all the horrible things reported in the news—child pornography, pissed off guys shooting dozens of strangers, moms drowning their babies in bathtubs. No, my own crap is proof enough for me. I know I'm a sinner. I can hide it pretty well, like Dr. Jekyll, but I know there's a Mr. Hyde lurking in the shadows.

Dr. Phil might pat me on the back and say, "Hey, give yourself a brake." But when I think about stuff I'm ashamed of, shrugging it off with "Nobody's perfect" doesn't help much. I could describe my dirty laundry, but I'll spare you that smelly experience. Suffice it to say I've been a very bad boy. Sure, I've tamed a few of my most visible flaws; but even grading on a curve, no way I'm passing the course.

Most people say, "I'm a good person." And why not? The high priests of the self-esteem cult incessantly preach a steady stream of narcotic ego-stroking messages for all to imbibe: *feel good about yourself; follow your dreams; tap into your unlimited potential; you can accomplish anything you want as long as you believe in yourself; indulge yourself... you deserve it.*

However, the Bible delivers a different message:

"I created you and gave you a beautiful environment to live in. I wanted you to enjoy your life with me as your companion and guide. But you chose to go your own way... with miserable results. I sent you prophets and teachers to help you understand the problem, but you were stubborn and refused to listen. I even clothed myself in human flesh in order to provide an ultimate solution to your dilemma. If you accept it, I will save you. If you reject it, there is no help for you. It's a matter of life and death."

The Bible is enough to convince me that I AM ADAM. I took the fall from paradise. I brought forth Cain and Abel and they continue to battle inside me. At least that's my condition. But hey—I don't know—maybe you're better than me. Maybe you have nothing to be sorry for, nothing to feel guilty about. But as for me, I've got lots of heavy baggage filled with dark memories I can't seem to unpack and discard. I've got old wounds that won't heal. For all of that—and more—I need forgiveness. I need God's mercy. I need Jesus.

"THERE IS NO EVIDENCE FOR the existence of God."

That's what I used to say back in high school when I flirted with atheism and parroted the lines you hear so often: *Science explains everything. We don't need a Creator.* I tried hard to embrace unbelief, especially since it would put no restraints on my behavior. But still, certain nagging questions bothered me: *Am I merely the accidental product of matter? And where did all this matter come from, anyway? Has it always existed? And how did it all go from inert stuff to a planet teeming with life? Did life emerge on its own from a primordial soup or was there a chef in the kitchen?*

I remember thinking, *"Obviously, something has always existed. How could something come from nothing?"* In my mind there were only two possibilities: life came from non-life (impersonal matter that has always existed) or life came from life (a deity who has always existed). Which was more rational? Well, you know the rest of the story. I eventually went with human beings coming from A DIVINE BEING.

The opposing view, now called "New Atheism," is currently in vogue. The books written by certain new, improved atheists proclaim, "Belief in God is more than unreasonable and unscientific—it is also a dangerous plague on mankind." It must feel delicious to join such an enlightened crowd and ridicule the poor dumb hicks who "check their brains at the door" while clinging to their silly superstitions. Actually, that's a pretty hard position to defend historically since men of faith have been some of the world's greatest thinkers, scientists and philanthropists. Nevertheless, I admit there are some Christians who check their brains at the door. I've seen my share. But are there some atheists who check their brains at the door? Again, I've seen my share.

Atheism is a belief system with it's own trinity of gods: matter, time and chance. Atheists must have faith that these three things have produced all that is, causing the improbable to become possible. To quote the Nobel prize-winning scientist George Wald, "Time itself performs miracles." If this is true, there is no such thing as good or evil, right or wrong, meaning, purpose or significance. Such a material god is silent, promising nothing, requiring nothing, giving no help, offering no peace, showing no mercy. And if matter is all there is, then nothing really matters. But most atheists don't live like that. They still try to be good people, care for their families, cry at movies and love their pets. Now when it comes to psychopaths—that's a different story—they really embrace the implications of atheism.

NOT TO SAY I DON'T have occasional doubts about it all.

Looking back, I sometimes wonder about God's methods. When I get depressed certain questions can float through my mind. *"With all due respect, Lord, couldn't you have given me clearer instructions? Couldn't you have kept me out of the cult? Why has my life been filled with so many ordeals?"*

Isn't that the crown-jewel argument against God? "How could a loving God allow pain and suffering in the world?" The existence of suffering does present a problem for believers. But unbelievers have an even bigger problem: they must explain the existence of everything else, the entire universe and, oh yeah, that includes pain and suffering. Well, I don't have an explanation for all the hardships and misery—I don't think anyone does—but I have to consider the proposition that God knows his business better than me.

It reminds me of when I was a kid. I hated shots. As soon as I saw the doctor's office I would start crying. My mother had to drag me out of the car as I screamed and clung to the door. My objective was to avoid pain; my mother's objective was to keep me healthy. After being held down by the nurse to get the job done, I would be pissed at my mom for hours. How could she do this to me? I was told the shots would keep me from getting sick later. But as a small child that assurance was beyond me. Nevertheless, it was true.

We're all like children who don't yet understand serious adult matters. Hold on—I take that back—we're more like unborn babies in the womb. We complain about the darkness and confinement, even kick about, but really we have no idea what it will be like when we are born.

I used to imagine myself going back in time to change some stuff. In my designer life, things would be different. I would replace the dysfunctional family I was raised in. I would never have been sucked into a cult. My disabled child would be healed. And my years of panic attacks and depression would be erased. But that was fantasy. When I face reality philosophically and spiritually, I accept that it has all been necessary to shape me into what I am meant to be. While I don't know why God allowed these things to happen, I can imagine him saying, "If I explained it to you, you still wouldn't get it. But you will. Just wait for your upgrade."

EIGHT YEARS IN THE CULT was quite a slice out of my life.

Why did I stay in for so long? I wish I had listened to Santiago, a young guy who came around to visit us in Peru. The Family fascinated him; so everyone took turns trying to get him to join up. But he was pretty smart and wanted to figure us out before making a commitment. I would often find him studying a stack of Mo Letters someone gave him. One night I noticed he was drawing a picture of our prophet, David Berg, propped up on a pedestal with members of the Family on their knees bowing down to him.

"Santiago, is that what you think of us?"

He gave me a quizzical look. "But he is your idol. ¿No?"

Santiago, Santiago...how right you were. We also worshipped the delusions created by David Berg: (1) We were in a special class because, unlike most Christians, we modeled ourselves after the original followers of Jesus who gave up their old lives and served God fulltime; (2) Because of our super-disciple status, we had a special connection to the Lord; (3) Therefore, God gave us a unique prophet with new and exciting revelations that would equip us to change the world.

These core beliefs made our community function. They also made us feel significant; in fact, we thought we were *legendary*. And you've probably picked up on something else: we were a proud bunch. But sadly the community itself became more important than the truth. If you can believe it, we used to chant: *My Family, my Family, right or wrong, my Family*. Reality was warped by our culture of songs, heroic anecdotes and charismatic meetings. Our familiar daily rituals provided shots of wellbeing. It was a romantic tale—a *tale* that wagged the dog.

Substance abuse leads to addiction. The Children of God supplied a powerful mind-altering substance that put me under the influence. And it turns out old delusions are hard to kill. Out of the Family, I subconsciously attempted to duplicate the sense of purpose the cult gave me. But alas, I no longer had a Rumplestiltskin to spin straw into gold. Ultimately my efforts came to a halt courtesy of panic attacks and clinical depression. My previous assumptions about myself were peeled away, layer by layer. I got a clear message: *You're not so different from everyone else, little man... not so special... not so enlightened after all.*

How did I get lured into the cult? It's not like I was kidnapped against my will. In fact, membership in the Children of God was not presented as a life of ease. No, we were told it would be a difficult, uphill battle with little to be gained materially. So way back in Austin when I contemplated joining the Family, I had a free choice—just not all the facts. I didn't think I was a blind devotee; but without doubt I had a serious visual impairment. I heard the Siren's alluring call and eagerly sailed toward her without watching for rocks beneath the ocean's surface. I rushed to the Family's fantasy with outstretched arms crying, "Take me. I'm yours!"

Cult members suffer from the "true-believer syndrome" because they persist in untenable beliefs despite evidence to the contrary. But just a casual stroll through the Internet is enough to convince me that most Homo sapiens are cultic creatures. After all, there is a humongous cult everyone is invited to join—the modern **cult**ure. It presents a pantheon of gods to worship. Magazine covers display doctored-up images of glowing celebrities for us to worship. These idols all proclaim they are the luckiest people in the world; they have found true love; they have finally found peace. *Don't you want the good life? Come on. Go for it!* It's hard to resist rushing toward this fantasy with outstretched arms crying, "Take me. I'm yours!"

There are plenty of things we run to: alcohol, drugs, sex, video games or the imaginary world of social media ("You like me! You really, really like me!"). We can entertain ourselves to death. It feels good for a while, like a sugar buzz, but when the high wears off...then comes the crash. It's tempting to join in with the other walking-dead zombies. It's like the lottery. We've heard the stories of big winners, so excited at first, only to have their lives ripped apart by all that money. But we keep on buying those tickets. Deep inside, don't we know better?

I read this article written by a journalist who knew several famous people before they became stars. She described them as ordinary folks until they hit it big. And then, as celebrities, they became self-centered and demanding—just plain difficult to be around. What caused this personality shift? The writer theorized that after chasing their dream and having it come true, they ultimately realized it had not produced the happiness they expected. Their circumstances might have changed, but fame had not changed them into better people. Disillusionment is a bitter pill.

Trent Reznor, founder of the music group Nine Inch Nails, was interviewed at the height of his success:

"Now I can play 200,000 seat halls instead of 2000 seat halls. I can go on MTV a thousand times a week rather than one time a month. Since I got everything I wanted I thought that maybe when I'd reached all these goals I'd find some sort of peace. But I didn't. And it looks like I'm more miserable now than I ever was."

You don't have to be famous to be bitten in the ass by reality. My own father was the most disgruntled successful person I ever knew. After leaving the Children of God I visited him often, trying to patch things up between us. We rarely spoke of my cult days, but one day he surprised me.

"Son, I can't understand why you ran off and joined that group."

"Well, I believed I was doing the right thing. It took time for me to learn I was wrong."

"But it was a cult. How could you fall for it in the first place?"

"You're right, dad. I fell for it. But don't we all fall for stuff? Even you?"

"I don't know what you're talking about."

"Well, you've been married 4 times. I think it's safe to say that every time you got married you thought you had found someone to make you happy. But so far all your marriages have ended in divorce. That's quite a pipedream. And you're a smart lawyer."

I thought he would be pissed; but he finally got a smirk on his face and chuckled.

"You know what?" he said, "You always were a little shit."

I didn't confide in him that my attraction to the cult had a lot to do with my desire for a happy family, including a father I could share my heart with, a father I wasn't afraid of. That would have been too much information. Years later, when his health began to fail and he was confined to a wheelchair, my father asked me to accompany him to the Mayo Clinic for a consultation with a specialist. One night I sat by his bed in the hotel room and he grabbed my arm.

"You've been married to the same woman for all these years. That's pretty amazing. I'm proud of you, son."

Then he started weeping. "The record of my life is a poor, scratched, banged up thing. I never thought I would end up like this."

I knew what he meant. The once powerful attorney was now an invalid, abandoned by all his wives, friends and many lovers. My father and I were more alike than we wanted to admit. We both pursued things that ultimately ended in bitter disappointment.

What could I do to pull out of my slump? Should I return to teaching? I needed a job, but worried about the stress. It was time for some cognitive therapy self-talk.

Mr. Negative:	"What if it all happens again? What if your depression returns?"
Mr. Positive:	"Come on. I can't let anxiety hold me down."
Mr. Negative:	"Maybe you're not ready to work again."
Mr. Positive:	"Or maybe it will be a snap, like riding a bike."
Mr. Negative:	"Dude, that bike analogy sucks."
Mr. Positive:	"You got a better one?"
Mr. Negative:	"Sure do. Are you ready to get back on the horse that threw you to the ground and stomped all over your ass?"
Mr. Positive:	"Hush! If I listen to you, I'll end up paralyzed on my couch again."

After going back and forth, I finally announced, "I'm going back to college."

12

1997 to the Present

I'm just a lowly frog under a spell
Cursed to live at the bottom of a well
I'm stuck in this place and long to be free
Here I must stay till the princess kisses me

THE END IS NEAR

WITH GREAT TREPIDATION I ENROLLED in a college class. That's right, just one. (Hey, I was taking it easy, testing the waters.) I thought it would be something to warm me up for re-entry into the work force. It was actually a wise decision because, after being a depressed hermit for over three years, it was harder than I thought. Even with such a light load, I almost quit several times when anxiety or depression threatened to return. But my cognitive therapy kicked in and when the darkness whispered to me, I talked back. *"What you're telling me is false. There's nothing wrong. So back off!"* By the time I finished that single class, things turned around. I still had to guard my thinking patterns, but my mind storms were more like bothersome winds instead of category 5 hurricanes.

On the campus I came across many students working on education degrees with plans to work in the public school system. I thought, *"Hmm… public school classrooms only contain a single grade level."* That sounded less stressful than what I had done for twenty years: teaching 3 grade levels in the same classroom. So, the public school grass was looking a little bit greener. However, to become a public school teacher, I needed a state teaching certificate. I gave it some thought and enrolled in a full load for the next semester. In a couple of years I finished all the credits required and passed the state examination with no problem. I was ready to go job hunting.

My first position fell in my lap. I had done some required student teaching in this little public school where over half the children came from low-income families. I enjoyed my time there and thought, *"This is the kind of place I'd like to work."* I had done a good job with the classroom teacher I had been assigned to and that was my ticket. When she heard a first-grade teaching position was opening up, she talked to the principal and I got the call.

During my years in the public school system I always used approaches from my Montessori background. I brought in all my Montessori equipment and the children absolutely loved it. In fact—probably not surprising—they appreciated the materials and the freedom of choice even more than my former private school students.

In the years that followed I taught first grade for quite a while, then kindergarten for a while, and finally second grade. Despite our culture's attempt to push elementary children into adolescence, I found second graders not much different from kindergarteners. When I tell people I worked with such young children, I have come to expect this question: *Weren't some parents worried about a man taking care of their babies?* But instead of expressing any such concerns, parents would often request that their child be placed in my class. Go figure.

Many of the children I taught just had one parent—often a single mom. Several times I was asked by such children, "Will you be my dad?"

As much as it touched my heart, I had to respond, "I can't. But I will be your friend."

Public school teachers are great to work with—just plain, hardworking folks. And although some of my methods were different, we got along fine. Occasionally a teacher would ask me to demonstrate my Montessori equipment. But despite my enthusiastic presentations, I made no converts.

It did my heart good to see kids happy to come to school. Many would actually groan when it was time to go home. I learned a long time ago that the key to children is to love and enjoy them. And children pick up on that. In the classroom I was having as much fun as the children. I saw a video once of a male lion with a few lion cubs jumping on him and biting his tail. That was kind of like me in the classroom.

One of the parents asked me, "How do you have the patience to work with little children all day?"

I said, "I have the best job in the world because I get to play with kids all day. Have you ever seen one of those old SPANKY AND OUR GANG movies? Well, I'm Spanky"

I couldn't read the children Bible stories or tell them about Jesus, but I tried to be a positive influence. When it came to elementary subject, teaching children to read was at the top of my list. But my aim was higher than mere mechanics; I wanted to give them a *love of reading*—a gift lasting a lifetime.

A teacher approached me once. "I can teach a child how to read, but I see your students actually love reading. How do you do that?"

The answer was easy. I made sure to read to the children every single day and put my whole heart into each book. I'm talking dramatic, full-body reading, changing my voice to match the characters and all the tricks of the trade. I knew I had done my job when the kids hauled their parents to the store to get their own copy of the book to read for themselves.

Most good books for children have something valuable to offer and I picked the very best. It always touched my heart when a child in my class would cry at the end of *Charlotte's Web* when the spider died. That's how sensitive they were. Once I was reading *The Lion, The Witch and The Wardrobe* and got to the part where the evil witch murders the great lion, Aslan. The children were shocked and demanded that I read the next chapter. When I read about Aslan coming back the life, a boy named Gerald exclaimed with excitement, "Hey! That's just like Jesus?" He never heard it from me; but I would have loved to be there when he related that story to his Jewish parents.

When the children had problems I had them come and talk it over. That was usually all it took. Usually we discussed the options and then I let them go to give it another shot. One day during recess I watched as two of my boys shunned a younger boy new to our class, not letting him join their games. Joey, the new kid, went and sat down under a tree and quietly sobbed. I called the two rascals aside for a chat.

"I see you two are doing all you can to make Joey sad. I'm sure he wishes he never came to this school. And that hurts my heart. He just wants to play, but he has no friends. You know, when I was in elementary school there was a boy who was really mean to me. One day he pushed me down and laughed when I got hurt. But a few days later he came up to me and said he was sorry. He said it made him feel bad that he had acted like a bully. After that we became good friends."

Then I walked away and went over to talk to Joey. Later I noticed the two offenders hadn't budged from where I left them. They just sat down and moped for the rest of recess. The next day one of their moms came to me with a twinkle in her eye.

"My son said he got in trouble yesterday. I asked him what he did and he told me he was being mean to the new boy. When I asked him what his teacher did about it, he got tears in his eyes and said, 'Mom, he just talked to us.'"

All through my school career I struggled with bouts of anxiety and depression. Most days I was into it, enjoying the flow; but I had my occasional pissy moods. When I blundered with a child, I learned early on to apologize. One day I misjudged a situation and corrected the wrong boy about making noise in the restroom. (He was one of the usual suspects, but that was no excuse.) When I found out the whole story I went to him and apologized.

"Will you forgive me?" I asked.

"Why not?" was his instantaneous response.

Parents frequently invited me to their homes for a visit. My young students—who believed I lived in my classroom—were always amazed to see me out of the school setting. It thrilled them to give me a tour of their home and introduce me to their siblings, pets and favorite toys. When the children saw me interacting with their parents, they got the message: we are all in this together. I made lots of friends that way, life-long friends. One such parent sent me a card in which she had written down different funny things her son had said about me. One of my favorites is: "I love my teacher. For sure I'm going to his funeral."

SOMETIMES I LEARNED MY OWN lessons during Story Time. Like the day I read aloud the fairy tale about the poor fisherman who caught a magical fish. The fish promised to grant a wish if he was set free. The fisherman went home and told his wife who said, "A fine new house would make me happy." The wish was granted. But the wife was not content. She demanded that her husband go back and ask the fish for more. Each time the fish granted the fisherman's request—even making the fisherman and his wife king and queen of the land—but still the wife was not content. Her last wish was to be GOD. When the magical fish heard that, all the wishes were taken away and the fisherman and his wife were returned to their original impoverished state.

At the end of the tale I asked the kids, "Do the things we want always make us happy?"

Nine-year-old Joshua piped up, "I know something that would make me happy for sure."

"What would that be, Josh?"

He smiled big, "If I only had a horse I would be happy."

I wondered how long Josh would hold onto that wish. How long did I hold onto my own wish—my own happiness horse. "If I only had a BIG WORK FOR GOD." But like the fisherman's wife, I was not content with what God had already given me.

Jesus told a story about a master who gave each of his servants a large amount of money to invest before going away on a long trip. When he returned, he asked each servant what profit had been made. When the master heard about a wise investment, he would say, "Well done thou good and faithful servant." More than anything, that's what I wanted to hear. But sadly, I wanted to give myself that accolade, to say it to myself, "Well done." I couldn't be at peace until I proved myself...to myself. When I fell short of my great expectations, I angrily punished myself with depression.

I was raised in a church with a hefty checklist of DOS and DON'TS. The Children of God ridiculed that as a "works trip." But ironically, the Family had its own righteousness checklist with one big item at the top: WORK FOR THE LORD. It was constantly on our minds: *Sure, God loves you, but what have you done for him lately?* We ended up feeling it takes plenty of good works to stay off of God's naughty list.

Naturally, God does care about what we do. (A Christian hit man? That's just not right.) But it's not as if we can earn God's love. It really is the other way around—any good we accomplish must flow from a loving relationship we already have with God. It's a lot like being married.

Doing things to please your spouse will not make you any more married than you already are.

Using that analogy, when it comes to my connection with God, I sometimes behave like an insecure wife. I start to have doubts about my performance and wonder if my husband still loves me. In this fretful state I try to think of ways to secure his love. When my husband sees my unhealthy state of mind, he comforts me by pulling out our marriage certificate.

"See there?" he says, "It's already settled between us. You don't need to worry."

***

IT TAKES TIME FOR CHILDREN to master even simple tasks. Along the way there are lots of trips and falls. As a teacher, my first job was to set up a stimulating learning environment. Even so, each child in my class was different and it took careful observation to identify individual needs. If a student wasn't making progress, the curriculum had to be altered to promote learning. The children never saw all the work I put into guiding them to success (nor would they have understood it if I explained it to them). I believe that's exactly how God is working for our benefit.

God is in charge of our curriculum. We might complain about the course of study, saying, *"Why do I have to learn this?"* But from God's point of view it's all about child development, doing what it takes to get his kids ready for graduation. He has set up a stimulating learning environment and watches over each student in his class. He knows what to do to help us become what we are meant to be. But since we don't see his plan, we are impatient and discontent with the process.

I wonder if young children realize the classroom is temporary. Sure, kindergarten is fun, but it's not meant to last. That's the same take I have on life—my time in God's classroom is limited. I should pay better attention to my teacher, but I'm easily distracted. If I could only get it through my thick head that this learning process is essential. Sometimes the lessons are hard and sometimes I need a bit of discipline for my own good. But I trust that my teacher knows best.

Young children often imagine what they will be when they grow up: *I want to be an astronaut.* We listen and smile, knowing their roles in life are really yet to be determined. But it's not just kids that do that. I can't believe I used to dream about becoming a HEAVY BROTHER in the Family. Thank God he woke me up and gave me something much better. My fiery-evangelist fantasy was replaced with the task of teaching children—and small ones at that.

I remember rejecting the idea of working with children because—after all—I wanted an important job. (Ain't that a laugh?) But God gently guided me to the profession that turned out to be a perfect fit for my personality. And for most of my adult life I have loved, cared for and prayed for hundreds of precious children. Through connections with their parents I've watched them grow up and have kids of their own. It has been a blessing that I did not deserve.

IT'S KIND OF AMAZING THAT Miriam and I are still together.

The odds were against us as we stumbled along—two steps forward and one step back. Despite some tumultuous years, we maneuvered through the marital obstacle course and made a discovery—we enjoy each other's company. Miriam is my best friend. I may not have given her the fairy tale romance she imagined in second grade, but our story did turn out to have a happy ending. She is my princess and I'm her frog prince. Warts and all, she loves me. And I love her back, even though her kiss has not turned me into a prince.

Here's some wisdom I'll throw in for free: to discover how thin your I'm-a-good-person veneer really is, just get married. I don't think there's another situation requiring more growth and change. Marriage ripped off my mask and exposed my weaknesses. It took a while, but God finally got it through my hard head: *This is the girl for you, your one true love.*

There was no way Miriam and I could foresee the challenge of raising a son with brain damage. But thank God we stayed together because it was definitely a job for both of us. We kept trying for more children, but it was not to be. Several years ago a gynecologist told Miriam that due to the structure of her uterus it was a miracle she ever conceived. The doctor said, "Well, that baby of yours was meant to be." Now that's something to ponder: God's gift of a disabled child.

At first Miriam and I worried about our son's future. When we enrolled Robin in public school, various specialists evaluated him to determine his needs. The tests indicated he had a low IQ, actually in the retarded range. This was hard to hear. We hoped things would improve after the successful removal of the brain tumor; but follow-up tests continued to paint a rather dismal picture.

But Robin has surprised everyone. As the years went by, he kept on developing cognitively. Although he remained under the special education umbrella, Robin managed to graduate from high school. He went from there into a vocational training program and went on to get a job he enjoyed. When we had him reevaluated, Robin's intelligence was in the average range. He does have challenges due to the brain damage—especially his obsessive-compulsive disorder—but he's not retarded after all.

As Christian parents we didn't want Robin to merely coast along on our convictions. So we prayed he would come to have faith of his own. As a teenager he struggled with many doubts; and then, like a flower blossoming, Robin developed a relationship with God. He often impresses us with spiritual lessons he is learning.

Recently he announced, "I have always been angry at all the bullies who made fun of me in school. But the Lord showed me I should forgive them. Then they can't bother me anymore."

"Wow, Robin! That's something I should do as well."

Unlike many other couples we knew, Miriam and I didn't have a bunch of kids. But we did have one, a special one, who has been such a blessing in our lives. Robin loves people and has a childlike enjoyment of the simple things in life. All who take the time to get to know him appreciate his sense of humor and his quirky knowledge on a variety of subjects.

It hasn't always been easy for us to watch our son bear the burden of his handicap. But we have a God who watched his own son suffer through life. And as we care for Robin, God cares for us. Sometimes it's hard, but not too hard. Through all the difficulties, God has instructed our hearts with many profitable lessons along the way. Miriam and I rejoice to have a God who patiently works with all of our own disabilities.

* * *

I'VE BEEN OUT OF THE Children of God for a long time.

I can't help but shake my head over the crazy things I used to believe. But do you know what encourages me? *Those first disciples!* You've got to love those guys. They were radical, leaving their old lives behind to follow Jesus; but even so, they were often clueless about his teachings and mission. They were all convinced Jesus would miraculously conquer the Romans and restore the kingdom of Israel. While they tagged along behind Jesus, they bickered about who would be more important in the future kingdom. Some were even bold enough to lobby Jesus for special future ranks.

The end of the Romans is coming! That was the huge error dominating their thinking. Here was Jesus, patiently correcting them, while they stubbornly clung to their misguided expectations. And here's the hilarious thing: when Jesus bluntly told them he would be put to death in Jerusalem, pick-of-the-litter Peter takes him aside and rebukes him for such an outrageous idea. Can you picture it?

"You've got it all wrong, Jesus. That will never happen!"

Jesus knew their misconceptions would eventually cause them to tumble headlong into confusion. The disciples all told him they would never desert him. *"We will die for you!"* But Jesus knew better. His followers didn't really know themselves very well. However, they soon got a clearer picture when soldiers hauled Jesus off to be executed. And the oh-so-brave band of brothers scattered.

I'm sure the disciples wondered, *"Were we wrong about everything?"* But failure is an excellent teacher. Is this sounding familiar? I was just like those mixed-up disciples. I loved Jesus, but I got lots of stuff wrong. The end of the world is coming! That was my misconception. And through it all, Jesus loved me anyway. Eventually I had a great fall and my weakness was exposed. After I picked myself up with painful bruises,

I was better for the experience.

Actually, I still believe the end is near, but not in the same way. Many years ago I pulled into a *Wal-Mart* and watched this elderly man in front of me having some difficulty getting his rather large car into a handicapped parking spot. As I waited I noticed a convertible behind me filled with four rowdy young men. The twenty-something driver honked and then screamed, "Come on! What's the holdup?"

After the senior citizen maneuvered into his space, I located a parking spot nearby and watched him slowly exiting his vehicle. The convertible with the youngsters pulled to a stop next to the aged gentleman and one of them shouted, "Don't you wish all old people would just die? I sure do!" The whole carload burst out laughing and then their driver revved his engine and sped off.

I was mortified for the old man and furious with the boys. I felt like getting in my car and chasing them down. But then it came to me: God's plan is perfect. Time flies for the foolish. Before those jerks knew it, they would also be old and honked at while driving along with their turn signal on. And who knows when God will require their souls? I hope they see the light because Jesus is coming soon... for each of them... for me... for you. Just give it a lifetime.

ONCE I GOT A SURPRISE phone call from a guy named Rick. In the Children of God his name was Watchman. He had been quite the big deal in the Family—a gifted songwriter, missionary pioneer and wheeling-dealing leader. He stayed in the group for about twenty years—a lot longer than me—and I could tell he was at the beginning stages of his own dark night of the soul. I was shocked when Rick told me what the Family had put him through. Over the next few months we exchanged letters and talked for hours on the phone. I encouraged him to get professional help and sent him some books on depression and cognitive therapy.

During one conversation Watchman told me he wanted to write an exposé of the cult based on his harrowing experiences. I tried to steer him away from that idea because I knew his head wasn't straight yet. He needed to take time to reflect and heal. But Watchman was undeterred. Like so many coming out of a cult, he wanted to throw himself into some kind of good work—something to justify his existence. He mailed me rough draft chapters for a while and then suddenly stopped. My letters to him went unanswered. About a year later I learned that Watchman committed suicide. I was greatly saddened because I felt in many ways we were kindred spirits, both struggling to make sense of it all, both trying to recover. Somehow he couldn't escape his deadly thoughts.

I still think of Watchman as I trudge along with my own stinking albatross of depression. But God helps me as I travel through many twisty pathways littered with my poor attempts to please Him. God's patience with me is beyond my understanding.

It has become increasingly clear that God's invisible hand has always been working behind the scenes to pull me out of the tough spots I get myself stuck in. When my focus was getting high on drugs all the time, God gave me something better. When I was held fast in the grip of the cult, God gave me a dose of reality. When my marriage was on a downhill slide toward divorce, God helped me come to my senses. And when I found myself incapacitated by anxiety and depression—down, down so low—merciful deliverance was provided at the bottom. In each of these situations God had a unique way of getting through to me. He is supremely inventive when it comes to creating escape hatches.

When I was seventeen years old, I sincerely asked God for guidance—to show me the way. But at the same time, I was blithely unaware of all the little false gods I adored. So first, God had to show me what was NOT THE WAY. I'm certainly not recommending cult membership as a wholesome spiritual exercise; but in my case, God flipped that mistake inside out and used it to shape me. It was a strange, counterintuitive answer to my prayer. And to be honest, I'm still being shown the way.

If I had not joined the cult, an infinite number of other bad choices were available. And knowing me, I could have easily botched things up even worse. I had to understand that I'm a broken guy in a broken world before God could put me in the shop and start the repairs. My experience in the Children of God gave me a clear picture of myself—quite a shocking one. But there is a divine influence on my heart in the midst of all my errors and despair. How long will it take for God to teach me to toss aside all the harmful things I clutch so tightly? I think a lifetime.

Some Final Thoughts...

AT FIRST I WAS CAUTIOUS about sharing my cult history. But when I did open up to friends, I was often surprised by their reactions. The main thing they heard was that I was in recovery from a distressing life event. In fact, many of them responded by telling me about their own traumatic experiences. "Sounds like my first marriage" or "Reminds me of when I sold Amway products." My story was a kind of metaphor for any disappointing life choice. And there was a common thread: *What we hoped would be great turned out to be a disaster.*

When I joined the Family I believed I had found the secret to a fulfilling life—a hidden treasure—and I gave up everything to obtain it. When that dream was smashed to bits, I spent many years down on the ground, picking up the shards, vainly trying to piece them together again. I was like an ex-convict, feeling out of place after being released from a long prison sentence. I had become institutionalized and missed my former inmates and the familiar prison routine. *"It was bad in there,"* I thought, *"but not all bad."*

Life in a commune has a way of tearing down social walls—no small talk is required in the tribe. In the Family we knew each other's stories; we ate together every day; we took care of each other's kids; we greeted each other joyfully with hugs and kisses. When I left the group I didn't know how to replace the rapport I shared with the group members. Relationships like that proved hard to duplicate. Years of counterculture damaged my ability to make social connections.

In the early 1980's I heard from others who split from the Family—some fed up with the weirdness, others kicked out for not swallowing everything. I tried to help because I knew they were in for a rough landing. Some got on with life, others crashed and burned, but no one left the cult unscathed. Depression was a common problem. I know of four ex-members who have committed suicide and I'm sure there are others I haven't heard about. I can relate because my depression almost killed me. I remain a member of MELANCHOLICS ANONYMOUS. "Hi, I'm John and I'm a melancholic."

Depression is painful, but pain can be a good thing if it alerts you to danger. My first onslaught of depression knocked me to the ground, but it also sent a signal: something is broken. I had to return to the God who loves me. It's easy for a father to love a child who fulfills his expectations, but what about loving a child who totally screws up? That love would have to be huge. That's what God offered me. It's amazing.

I've been told the Children of God is disbanded—no more communal colonies, no more literature sold on the streets, and no more using sex to gain converts. But this is an old shape-shifting trick. They have morphed into an online organization masquerading as a nice Christian group (donations are welcome). Who runs it? Maria, David Berg's successor, who gained power and influence the longer she stayed with Mo. She claims to be a great prophetess and has worked hard to edit out the excesses of the Family's sordid history. *"Oh, we were all just young radicals back then and made many mistakes. We are different now!"* Really? I'm sure that underneath the makeover, it's still the same house of lies.

It takes a charismatic con artist to form a cult. Cult leaders skillfully take advantage of people searching for answers. Cults claim to provide something you lack. Feeling inferior? Cults make you feel part of a superior group. Feeling lonely? Cults give you an instant supply of friends and family. Have a desire to serve God? Cults will fan that flame into an all-consuming blaze.

Many went through hell in the Family. I've read several books by ex-members who detail their heartbreaking experiences. Their message comes through loud and clear: **EVIL CULT BAD!** I can't argue with that. But I do have a concern: I'm afraid some of these books describe cults nobody would ever want to join, much less stay in for years. I was in the Children of God for eight years; others were in for decades. So obviously, cults offer something attractive. Otherwise, who would give them the time of day?

In the Family we would link arms and sing, "Behold how good and how pleasant it is for the brethren to dwell together in unity." And it was true; it was good. Despite all the lies we were fed, there were many positive things we experienced: love, dedication, self-sacrificial service. We joined the Family because we thought it had something that couldn't be found elsewhere. And that is one reason why I decided to share my personal story—to illustrate the allure of good things mixed with evil.

My brief history is not as exciting or tragic as other cult testimonies I've heard. In fact, I'm sure some will think I've been too soft on the Children of God. But I just wanted to tell what happened to me in that eight-year slice. That's all I've got. I haven't been able to include a bunch of shocking stories about the notorious top leadership because, honestly, I was never that high in the food chain. What's more, the really bad stuff happened after I dropped out of the group. In the years after my escape, I heard reports of some alarming things going on in the Family. I shouldn't have been surprised since the flaw was in the pattern from the start. Still, I never imagined it would get so messed up.

In trying to capture the person I was, I had to stretch my memory back to the 1970's; so I'm sure I didn't get every detail right. But I did have an advantage—a shoebox full of journal notebooks to help me present a fairly accurate picture. I didn't set out to write a self-help success story. With all I've been through, I don't feel so successful. But during the writing process I discovered quite a bit about that 17-year-old who found God, the 18 year old who joined the Family, the 26 year old who struggled after exiting the group, the 41 year old who collapsed under the weight, and the 68 year old who has absorbed them all. I'm a rather poor version of Jacob in the Bible. I wrestled with God's angel and have limped along ever since—somewhat lame, but grateful to be on my feet.

ABOUT THE AUTHOR

*John Titus is a native Texan, therapeutic journalist,
meditative poet and optimistic melancholic.
You may contact him with questions and comments at
his website, where you will also find a link to his social media.*

www.trippingup.net